UNFINISHED

Failure Does Not Equal Finished

By Randall Popham

Sarah we are
blessed by you!
Randall Popham

TABLE OF CONTENTS

DEDICATION

I dedicate this book to my loving wife, Dana, who has been a constant encouragement from the first day I met her. Thank you, Dana, for always encouraging me to write and share the things God puts on my heart. Your vision of my writing being like a never ending flow of ink coming from a feather pen has been a continuous reminder of the work God wants to do through this task. Thank you for all the times you protected my schedule and encouraged me to get away and write even though it meant time away from you and our children. You have been a vital part of this book, and I could not have written it without your love and support. Thank you. I love you.

ACKNOWLEDGMENTS

I have sincere and profound gratitude to all the amazing people who have helped me accomplish this project. I want to thank Kathrine Lee for believing in me and coaching me on this journey. Your honest and wise feedback has always been given with unbelievable encouragement. Each conversation with you breathed more life and passion into me. You make me want to keep writing. Everyone needs people like you in their life.

I also want to acknowledge the loving and supporting people of Lanier Hills Church. Thank you for always supporting and encouraging me to write. Thank you to all of my amazing church staff for using your gifts and talents to serve the body and allowing me to use my gifts to help the body in the way that God created me. To the supportive and encouraging Elders of Lanier Hills Church, thank you for your blessing on the writing of this book.

Thank you, Scott Goetz, for telling me dozens of times over the years that I should be writing. Whenever writing gets hard and the words aren't coming to my mind, I hear your voice in my head telling me to write. Thank you also for your personal coaching and holding me accountable to finish this book. I couldn't have completed it without you.

I also want to thank the countless individuals who have trusted me enough to allow me to speak into their lives over the years. Your stories and struggles have given me the experience to speak to others through this book. Thank you for allowing me to be a part of what God was doing in your life.

I can't make a list of people I want to thank and not include my parents Tommy and Susan Popham. Thank you for breaking generations of addictions and destructive behavior in our family and setting me on a new path. Thank you for believing in me as a young man and allowing me to chase after every dream. I can't tell you enough how proud I am to be your son. I wish every person had the privilege to have parents as amazing as you. I love you.

Last but not least, I want to thank my wife and my children for their unwavering love and support for writing this book. The extra hours and days away from you outside my regular time pastoring have not been easy for any of us. I love being with you more than anything in the world. Thank you for encouraging me to finish. I love you. – Randall

INTRODUCTION

Have you failed? I mean really failed? Have you failed so bad you feel like giving up? Then this book is for you. This book is for every person who has failed and wants to know if God will forgive them, if God still has a plan for them and how to turn their loss into a win. This book is for...

People wanting to overcome their failures.

People battling addictions.

People who are recently divorced and wondering if God is finished with them.

The leader who failed miserably and wonders if he/she will ever lead again.

People who keep missing their own goals.

People who've been fired, laid off or failed at a business.

People who've failed at relationships.

People that keep failing at keeping promises to God.

People who walked away from God.

People wanting to give up and quit trying.

People afraid to set goals because of the fear of failure.

People who want a better future than they had before they failed.

If any of the above describe you, then this book is written for you. In the short time it will take you to read this book, you'll discover that you are not alone and that there's hope for you. You'll learn how God uses your failure for good and you'll master the steps you have to take to bounce back.

First of all, I wrote this because I believe God wanted me to. I believe He was telling me to write it even if no one ever reads it. In some sense, this title is a personal achievement for me of a failure in my past. I failed the eleventh grade in high school ironically because I didn't want to write a paper and present it to my class. The finishing of this work is proof to me that past failures do not define your future. It has been a long (much longer than I expected) journey of writing this book. I almost quit multiple times, and the only way I could finish was to write a friend a large check and tell him to give it to an organization we both dislike if I didn't meet my deadline. Thank God I finished on time!

I also wrote this for you. I wrote this because I care about maltreated and dejected people. I care about the people who I have sat with countless times who shared their stories of failure with me. Almost weekly, I talk with people who have messed up and failed in some area of their life, and they have a hard time seeing past their failure. This book is about giving hope to people who feel hopeless. It's about empowering people to keep pressing on no matter how bad they've failed.

I've written this as a handbook for helping individuals who have failed to get back on track with God's help. This book is a mix of honest stories and Biblical examples of people who have walked through failure. It's also full of scripture to guide you as you take this journey of recovery and healing.

There are five sections with several subsections in each. I've included a couple of questions at the end of each subsection to help you slow down, think and consider what God wants to say.

There are several ways you could use this book. Feel free to use it however you like. You may choose to sit down and read it through without stopping and then go back and reread it with the questions. You can also use it as a personal devotional. There are twenty-four short subsections with questions you could use for several weeks if you decided to do one per day. Or you can use it for a five-week small group study. There are questions at the end of each section that you can use for group questions. As you are reading, you may think of a friend that needs to hear the message contained on these pages. Please share it and together let's help other people find a way forward.

If you are ready to move beyond your failure or wondering if you even can, then this is for you. There's no need to delay any longer. Turn the page and let's get started on your path to recovery.

CHAPTER 1

WELCOME TO THE CLUB

"We are all failures-at least the best of us are."
- J.M. Barrie[1]

FAILURE IS UNIVERSAL

I couldn't breathe. The stiff punch to my gut from the pubescent bully up the road took more than my breath. It stole my pride. My middle school dreams of being liked and popular crashed to the ground as the kids on the bus laughed out the window. I lay there in the midst of my subdivision, cradling my stomach, and wishing it would all go away. I failed to hold my tongue to a teacher about the bully who skipped school, and he was not going to let me forget about it. I didn't forget about it. I'm forty-three now and the pain of that day still lingers with me.

That day, I failed to stand up to the bully. I failed to protect my precious ego. I failed, and there is nothing like lying on the ground with grass in your teeth and the crippling sound of teen laughter to remind you that you failed. That evening, I determined not to let that ever happen again. I started lifting weights. I watched Rocky movies. I got a new haircut. I grew tougher and developed an attitude that I could do anything and achieve anything.

That attitude will carry you a while, and it seems every young high school graduate, college graduate or new young employee has that attitude. But, life has a way of humbling us and bringing us all to our knees in brokenness. This book is for those who've also ended up on their knees with their dreams, plans and hopes crushed like a middle school ego. This book is for "failures." It is for me.

No one grows up wanting to be a failure, but we all end up

there at some time and in some areas of our lives. When the realization that you've failed hits you like a punch to the gut, it feels like it takes years off your life instantly. I know. I've been there, and so have you, or you wouldn't be reading this book.

This morning, I'm sitting in a parking lot writing the opening to this book after failing for four weeks to write. I'm fighting feeling like a failure for not being four weeks ahead of where I am today. While writing here in my car, I received a heartbreaking phone call, giving me more urgency and purpose to write. A close friend whose hidden life of abusing prescription painkillers took a drastic change last night. He was supposed to start a great new job today. Instead, his wife is taking him to a drug treatment center as I type. His children will all find out he's an addict. His friends and parents from whom he hid this addiction will find out. The job he was supposed to start this morning is gone. His life will never be the same. He failed.

Failure is universal. It happens to us all at a given point in time and in certain areas of our lives. When failure happens, it's people like my friend—like you and me - who end up in my office, seeking Pastoral help. Almost weekly, I hear the heartbreaking stories of failed marriages, crushed dreams, and broken promises. They all have the same emotions—fear, anger, brokenness, and doubt. It's no secret—failure hurts. In my office, there is a constant flow of tissue boxes used by the many hurt hearts and broken egos that come seeking help. If I've learned anything as a Pastor, it is that failure is universal.

If you've failed, welcome to the club. You've been a member your whole life and you didn't know it. You fit right in with the rest of us. If you don't think you are part of the club, then you need to get a glimpse of yourself from God's point of view. The Bible says this about you and me, "No one is righteous—no not one!" (New International Version, Rom 3:10)

God says no one is perfect. No one is perfect in every area of his or her life. You may have been successful in some, but when it comes to always doing the things God wants you to do, you have failed. I bet right now you can probably think of a time when you did something and you knew it was wrong. You failed. It may be that thing that you failed at that has caused you to read this book.

If we all have failure in common, then there is another thing we also have in common. It's the question: "Am I finished?" Time after time, I've sat with the hurting and wounded, who've bravely found their way into my office after they've failed. You can read it on their face and see it in their tears. They've lost hope, lost sight of the future and run out of courage. They ask, wanting to know "Is God done with me?" They can't see beyond their disappointment. They can't imagine a future better than their past. They are emotionally bruised, mentally stuck and spiritually crushed. Each come looking for hope, and the good news is—there is hope. God's not finished. He's still working and He still has a plan.

QUESTIONS

1. What difference does it make for you to know that everyone has failed?

2. What makes your failure(s) different from anyone else's?

WHAT IS FAILURE?

There's nothing like a big red "F" across the top of a paper to let you know you've failed. That huge terrifying "F" means "failure." The student failed the test. He or she didn't meet the standard and now it's etched on the paper, in the grade book and in their minds. The humbling feeling of receiving an "F' is one I was too familiar with in High School. I didn't just fail a test or class. I failed the 11th grade. Ironically, I failed because I didn't want to write a paper. On the first day of my 11th Grade Literature class, the teacher made us all stand in groups of threes. Then she made two people from each group sit down. The ones left standing represented the percentage of people who would fail the class. I was one of the ones left standing. I remember thinking, "This is not right. This is rude. I'll show her!" No one was going to label me as a failure.

Right up front, she let us all know what it would take for us to pass the class. To pass the class, we were required to write a large paper and present it to the class. The entire semester revolved around the paper. If you failed the paper, you failed the class. If you failed the class, you could not move on to your senior year of High School.

At that time in my life, schoolwork was not a priority. I was busy working, having fun and focusing on my active social life. I made little time to work on a paper. I filled my schedule with many things, but writing a paper was not one of them. The first deadline was coming soon and I could feel its weight. I remember thinking I could just cram it all in the night before it was due. I did it before. I could do it again.

The night before the first important deadline was due, I sat down at my parent's kitchen table to write. It was 10 PM. I had completed no previous work and had none of the material I needed to write a paper. I remember the feeling of looking at the empty pages and thinking "I'm going to fail. I'm going to be one of the ones the teacher said would fail." I tried writing, but it was no use. At 2 AM, I still had nothing. At that moment, it sunk in. I would fail the class, and I would fail the 11th Grade. All my friends would move on without me. I wouldn't just get a red "F" on a paper; I would be labeled a failure. Just like the teacher predicted, I did fail the class and I failed the 11th grade. I failed to meet the standard set by the teacher, and I failed.

"Failure is something you do. It's not who you are."

I felt like a failure every day of the next school year. I was reminded daily that I failed when I showed up at school and checked into an 11th grade homeroom, again. Each weeknight, I had to attend a class forty-five minutes away from my home while also taking a full schedule of senior year classes just to graduate with my class. That long daily drive gave me lots of time to think about my failure. It was not the senior year I hoped to experience. I was labeled a failure. I felt like a failure.

We all know what it feels like to experience failure. We experience it regularly. Do a Google search for the definition of "Failure" and you'll get the meaning — "A lack of success."[1] However, you don't have to look it up to know what it is. We know what failure is. It's missing the mark we or someone else sets for us. When we don't reach that mark we fail. When we fail, we know it.

We could all make a long list of the things of which we've failed. Fill a room full of people, and you will be in a room filled with individuals who've missed the mark. You won't have to look hard and dig deep to discover we've all missed it somewhere in life. You'll find people who've failed at relationships, careers, personal goals, promises to God, addictions, parenting, leading, holding our tongue and many other things. The list could go on and on.

There's not a person on earth who hasn't failed. The Apostle Paul says, "For everyone has sinned; we all fall short of God's glorious standard." (New Living Translation, Rom 3:23)[2] According to the Bible, "everyone" failed to meet God's high standard for living right. That may seem insensitive and uncaring, but it's no secret to God, you or the world. You've failed. Yes; you, me, your sweet Mom and everyone else you know has failed. We may be a success at some things but failures at others, and we aren't hiding our failures from God.

In some areas of your life, you've received an "F." You missed the mark and you feel like you are walking around with a big red "F" on you right now. It's imprinted on your heart, mind and emotions. It feels like a label you'll wear for the rest of your life. It could be, but it doesn't have to be. Failure is something you do. It's not who you are. You have missed the mark but you haven't missed the opportunity for God's grace.

QUESTIONS

1. What are some of your failures that you remember the most?
2. Which of your failures has been the hardest to overcome?

YOUR BROKEN HEART

The effects of failure on our mind, will and emotions a. powerful. Even if you've been successful in most parts of your life, it only takes one big meaningful failure in one area to make you feel like a failure in all areas. I have a friend who is one of the most successful people I know. It seems everything he touches turns to gold. He has real estate and businesses all around the United States. He has more classic cars in his garage than all the cars my wife and I have ever owned in our lifetime. He's a success in the eyes of many, but that didn't keep his broken heart from ending up in my office, tearfully describing how his marriage failed.

My friend's marriage of thirteen years came to a halt when his wife and stepchildren walked out the door. He tried to ignore the pain of his failed marriage for several years after his divorce, but his unresolved failure continued to eat away at him. The effects of his failure tormented his mind, will, and emotions. That's what eventually led him into my office where he cried and wept for several hours as he told me his story. The powerful effects of failure left him broken and feeling useless. This successful man felt like a failure. His heart was crushed.

My friend's story isn't uncommon. Meaningful failures have a powerful psychological impact on us all. According to Guy Winch in his book, "Emotional First Aid," there are three ways meaningful failures affect us. "Failure inflicts three specific psychological wounds that require emotional first aid. It

17

...mages our self-esteem by inducing us to draw conclusions about our skills, abilities, and capacities that are highly inaccurate and distorted. It saps our confidence, motivation, and optimism, making us feel helpless and trapped. And it can trigger unconscious stresses and fears that lead us to inadvertently sabotage our future efforts."[1]

My friend was experiencing all three negative effects of failure. His self-esteem was damaged. He had an inaccurate view of himself, and he felt hopeless. Failure does that to us. It makes us have false views of ourselves. It makes us feel hopeless, and it can set us off in a spin of self-induced failures.

> **"If your spirit is crushed by failure, God is closer to you now than He's ever been."**

Failure goes straight to the heart. It runs deep and impacts us at all levels. It can sap the life out of you and set you on a path of continuous pain. That's one of the reasons God warns us to protect our heart. In Proverbs 4:23, God says, "Above all else, guard your heart, for everything you do flows from it." (NIV)[2] All you do flows from your heart, and when you experience failure, your heart is exposed. A broken and exposed heart needs help. It needs healing. It needs to find hope. Thankfully, the God of the Bible is a God of hope.

If your heart is broken, you are in a good place. You are in a good place because God is close to you. Psalm 34:18 says, "The LORD is close to the brokenhearted and saves those who are crushed in spirit." (NIV)[3]

If your spirit is crushed by failure, God is closer to you now than He's ever been. He may seem silent or uncaring at the moment. You may even think He's mad at you. But, He is close. He's very close. He's working in your life and He has a purpose for your pain.

If you feel discouraged by your failure, God wants to give you the courage to move forward. Your success and happiness in life will be determined by how you respond to your failure. Author and Leadership guru, John C. Maxwell, says this about responding to failure, "The difference between average people and achieving people is their perception of and response to failure."[4] God is close to you in your failure. God is for you, and He wants to turn your loss into a win. He wants you to have the courage to move forward and let Him redeem your failure. He wants to heal your broken heart. You may feel like you are finished, but God is just getting started.

QUESTIONS

1. What emotions and beliefs do you experience whenever you fail?
2. How does it make you feel to know that God is close to you when your heart is broken by failure?

GETTING BACK UP

David was a close friend in high school. He was big, mean and strong. It's nice having those kinds of friends in High School until he wants to go head to head with you in football drills. I'll never forget the day at our freshman football team practice when I had to try to tackle David in a one-on-one tackling drill. Like I said, David was big and strong. I was big, but David was bigger and stronger. David could run the ball well, but he didn't have to sprint. He would just lower his shoulder and run right over you like a bull charging a red flag.

Run right over me is what David did. On the first try, I attempted to tackle David high. That didn't work. I ended up flat on my back. The word for that type of hit is "Pancaked." David flattened me like a pancake.

I asked the coach to let me try again. I tried again. This time, I got lower. Same result. I ended up on my back, but this time around, my ego was hurt too. I jumped back up and asked to do it again. David said, "Randall, don't do it again." I said, "I'm doing it again!" The coach obliged.

David lined back up across from me. He held nothing back and came at me with everything he had. It felt like it too. I ended up on my back, bruised and battered with the football team watching. Humiliated and mad, I jumped back up and said, "Let me do it again!" David just shook his head and the coach sent me to the back of the line. I never tackled David that day but I've never forgotten the lesson I learned.

Recently, David and I talked about that day at practice. I've never forgotten it. He remembers it too. He still had an evil laugh as we reminisced about that day. I didn't achieve the goal of tackling David, but something in me rose to the occasion and said no matter how many times I get knocked down, I'm going to get back up.

Get back up! That's what you have to do when you've failed. We all fail in our attempts, but the only way to truly fail is to quit trying. The

"The only way to fail is to quit trying."

Bible says, "The godly may trip seven times, but they will get up again. But one disaster is enough to over through the wicked." Proverbs 24:16 (NLT)[1]

Did you see what that verse says? It says godly people get back up when they fail. Notice what it doesn't say. It doesn't say godly people don't fail. For some reason, we think good people don't fail. Good-hearted people fail all the time. The question is, will you jump back up and try again? Or will you be person who is destroyed by one disaster?

You are going to get "pancaked" from time to time in this life. You'll get the wind knocked right out of you. You may see little stars and wonder what hit you.

Perhaps you are flat on your back now. You are humiliated, hurt and not wanting to even get out of bed. Everything in you is screaming, "Don't get up." But you have to! God is not finished with you. There is still more to your story. I said it before and I'll say it again — The only way to fail is to quit trying. Keep getting up!

If you are reading this book, it's probably because you've failed. You may be at a very low point in your life, and you are only hanging on by a thread. Maybe your failure isn't huge but it is habitual and the constant failure has eaten away at your soul.

If you are seeking to make some kind of sense out of your failure, I wrote this book for you. God is near to you and He's up to something good in your life. As you read through the rest of the book, I pray you'll break free from any lies you may be believing and that you'll find hope. I pray you'll get back up and let God make something beautiful out of your mess.

QUESTIONS

1. What's the difference between people who stay down when they fail and someone who gets up when they fail?

2. How many times should someone fail before it's okay not to get back up?

CHAPTER 2

FAILURE'S DECEPTION

Failure is a detour, not a dead-end street.

-Zig Ziglar[1]

HURT EGO. VULNERABLE MIND.

When we fail, we have many raw emotions and countless thoughts that can't always be trusted. I observed this recently when a young couple came to visit me in my church office. I wasn't sure why we were meeting. They said it was urgent and we quickly worked them into my schedule. I knew they were active members of our church, but I wasn't sure why we were meeting until they sat down. Their body language immediately gave it away. Their crossed arms, their red eyes and the three feet of space between them told me they were having marital issues.

I guessed right. Within the first minute of the conversation, I was told the wife had been having an affair. She was broken. He was broken. They were genuinely hurting. The pain of their failing marriage was evident in their faces and words. She loved her husband, and he loved her but he was married to his work and her loneliness led her to look for attention in other places. It only took one extremely friendly coworker to show her the attention she was craving, and she gave in. The affair had been going on for months until he found out and she confessed. Their world was crumbling around them, and they were broken-hearted.

The pain of their failed marriage drove them to meet with me. They were looking for hope and looking for answers, but her mind wouldn't let her see beyond her failure. We talked, and they shared how they still loved one another and wanted to stay married. His love for his wife was evident and shocking. He was still broken but ready to forgive and willing to do whatever it took to fix their marriage. He recognized his role in their failing marriage and was ready to do whatever he could to fix it.

She was quiet and tearful as we talked about the failing marriage. She recognized her failure and the pain she caused her husband. Together, we all talked about a path forward but I could tell she was still carrying something heavy in her soul. As we wrapped up the time together, I asked her if she wanted to say or ask anything. It was then she revealed the huge weight that was hanging on her heart like a battleship anchor. She looked at me and began to cry. With tears streaming down her face and with a sincere desperation, she asked me: "Will God ever forgive me?"

"Will God ever forgive me?" That's a question many of us ask when we morally fail. Our sense of fairness and justice can't understand how God could forgive our massive blunders or our outright disobedience. When we are hurting and reeling from our failures, our emotions are unstable and our thinking is vulnerable. Our mind goes to dark places and we can rarely see clearly. Our thinking gets muddy, and we struggle to tell the truth from a lie.

In our vulnerability, we often make false assumptions about God. When we fail big time or fail over and over again, we are tempted to assume "God is good. I am not. Therefore, God is finished with me." That's what my broken-hearted friend sitting across from me was thinking. By asking, "Will God ever forgive me?" she was saying, "God is good. I am not! He must be finished with me!" She couldn't see how God could still love her

25

or have a future for her.

You and I are just like my friend. When we fail, we are tempted to think our failures are fatal. We believe deep down that our Failure = Finished. We say things like this to ourselves…

THE FAILURE and THE LIE

The failure: "I'm divorced."
The Lie: "I'll never be happily married again."

The Failure: "I got fired."
The Lie: "No one will ever hire me now."

The Failure: "I've gained my weight back."
The Lie: "I'll never be healthy."

The Failure: "I gave in to my addiction again."
The Lie: "I'll never be free."

The Failure: "I failed to reach my goal."
The Lie: "I'll never be successful. I'll just give up."

The Failure: "I failed morally in ministry."
The Lie: "I'll never be able to serve a church again."

The Failure: "I broke a promise to God."
The Lie: "God is finished with me."

The Failure: "I walked away from God."
The Lie: "God will never receive me back again."

Our hurt egos and vulnerable minds will believe just about anything when we are down. It's during those dark and desperate times we have to see through the muddy thinking and understand the truth. When you read the Bible and understand how God deals with our failures, you begin to realize that with God, failure does not equal finished.

Your failures are not fatal and you are not finished. As long as you're breathing and your heart is still beating, God is not finished with you. You may have failed, but it doesn't mean you're finished. God's hasn't given up on you. The Bible clearly and consistently describes God's mercy and compassion for you even when you fail. Lamentations 3:22-23 states, "The steadfast love of the Lord never ceases; his mercies never come to an end; they are new every morning; great is your faithfulness." Lamentations 3:22-23 (English Standard Version)[1]

God is not finished. He is the God of many merciful mornings. His love has not ceased, and His mercies have not run out. He has a whole new load of mercy for you today. Your hurt ego may not feel it and your vulnerable mind may not see it, but your failure does not equal finished.

QUESTIONS

1. Which lies are you tempted to believe about yourself and your future when you fail? Write them down.
2. Read Lamentations 3:22-23. What do these verses tell you about God's love and mercy?

FAILURE ≠ FINISHED

AGREEING WITH THE ENEMY

My wife and I occasionally have the hardest times agreeing on a place to eat during our dates. It's not that we have different tastes. We actually like a lot of the same foods. But, sometimes, we just can't decide what type of food we are in the mood to eat. We will play the familiar game of "What do you want to eat? I don't know. What do you want to eat?" We've even driven around and around our town trying to come to an agreement on a place to eat. When we finally agree on a place, there is instant harmony and we set out toward that destination.

There's power in agreement. It sets the course and the destination at which we will end up. In life, we often make agreements and depending with whom the agreements are made, those decisions can have a positive or negative impact on our lives. We also make agreements with ourselves. It seems I make an agreement with myself every morning about what I will or will not eat that day. I rarely keep that agreement. Nevertheless, at least I try.

Some agreements are more dangerous than others. The most destructive agreements we can make are the ones we make with spiritual forces we cannot see. We cannot see them, but we are tempted to agree with them daily. The Bible clearly states that there are spiritual forces constantly waging war against us. The Apostle Paul says this in Ephesians 6:12, "For our struggle is not against flesh and blood, but against the rulers, against the authorities, against the powers of this dark world and against the spiritual forces of evil in the heavenly realms."[1]

Every day, we face a barrage of spiritual forces. These forces have one goal in mind—DEATH. They target your dream, your purpose, and your life. Our enemy is a thief and he aims to steal your life. The Bible makes it very clear, "The thief comes to steal, kill and destroy." John 10:10 (NIV)[2]

"Your failures only become fatal when you believe you are finished."

The enemy intends to steal your influence, take your life and destroy your dreams. He wants you to give up, quit and die. If he can get you to believe you are finished, he'll be successful. Our invisible enemy is "the father of lies" John 8:44 (NIV)[3] and his native tongue is Lying. He is a master at feeding us the lies we want to hear, and he knows the opportune time to speak them.

When you've failed and you're hurting, the enemy knows exactly what to say to get you to agree with him. When you've failed and you're at your lowest, the enemy speaks these words: "You are finished." It's at that point we are tempted to make a tragic mistake and agree with the enemy. If you agree with the enemy, you'll end up at his destination. You'll get his results. Follow the agreement to the end, and you'll get the death of your dreams, your influence and ultimately your life.

Your failures only become fatal when you believe you are finished. We can look all around us and see those who believe they are finished. They've stopped dreaming. They've stopped trying. Some have stopped living.

It is not always one failure that leads to destruction. Often, it's the tiny failures that happen over and over again that get us. They are like paper cuts. One paper cut isn't so bad, but thousands of paper cuts can become fatal. My friend, Kathrine Lee, calls it "Death by paper cuts." The Master of Lies is exceptionally good at convincing us that our multiple mini-failures mean we are finished.

I'll never forget the phone call I received, telling me that a former co-worker, friend and ministry leader had given into the enemy's lies. I remembered him as a bigger-than-life individual. He was strong, handsome and gifted. He influenced hundreds of thousands of people in their walk with God through his ministry, but my friend had a secret he hid from everyone. He was addicted to pornography and was a sex addict. He lived a secret life of sexual addiction and when his secret was revealed, he lost his ministry and eventually his beautiful family. His world came crashing down around him. He was at his lowest point, and that's when he made a tragic agreement with the enemy. He couldn't see a future past his failure, and he agreed he was finished. His agreement with the enemy eventually led him to the destination the enemy intended all along. He took his own life.

The enemy also has a scheme to take your life. The Apostle Peter warns us, "Be alert and of sober mind. Your enemy the devil prowls around like a roaring lion looking for someone to devour." 1 Peter 5:8 (NIV)[4]

A lion loves to attack the weakest and most vulnerable of the herd. He sneaks in, waits for the right moment and pounces on his prey. Our enemy knows our vulnerable moments. He knows when we fail and he's ready to feed you a lie when you are weak. He'll try to get you to agree that your failure equals finished.

Do you believe you are finished? Have you been making agreements with the enemy? What agreements have you made with the enemy about your failure? I encourage you to break your agreements with the enemy. Before you read any further, stop and ask God to reveal any agreements you've made with the enemy about you or your future. Use a piece of paper to list your failures. Then beside them, write down what you've been feeling and believing about this failure. Ask yourself if this belief is from God or the enemy? Here's how you'll know. If it's from the enemy, it will be fatalistic. You'll not see any good, hope or future beyond the failure. If it's from God, you'll see hope, grace, and a future beyond your failure. When you identify an agreement you've made with the enemy, break the agreement. Declare out loud and write on the paper, "This agreement is not true, and in the name of Jesus, I break the agreement."

You're not finished! God still has a plan and purpose for you. Your failures will only become fatal when you believe you are finished.

QUESTIONS

1. How would you describe an "agreement that is made with the enemy?"

2. Can you think of at least three agreements you've made with the enemy about your failure?

IF YOU THINK YOU'RE FINISHED.

The danger of believing failure-equals-finished is that it becomes a self-fulfilling prophecy. If we believe we are finished, we usually end up being finished. Our beliefs about our failure have a direct impact on how successful we will be in the future. "Over 50 years ago, psychologists Martin Seligman and Steve Maier gave participants a test and told them it was indicative of intelligence—it was not. In fact, the test was rigged such that it was impossible to complete. They found that once participants failed at the (rigged) test, they acted helpless, so much so that when they were given a similar test, one that was well within their capacities, they failed at it—because they felt too helpless to give it a real try. Failure often makes us feel helpless even though we are not."[1] If you believe you're finished, it's highly unlikely you'll succeed in the future.

> "The danger of believing failure-equals-finished is that it becomes a self-fulfilling prophecy."

Believing you aren't a failure is crucial for future success. I've coached all my kids in basketball, football, baseball and softball. In each of those sports, there are usually more failures than there are successes. One of the hardest and most important things to teach kids is that when they fail, it doesn't mean they are failures. My oldest son played quarterback for his football team.

It's a stressful position. The quarterback is the coach on the field. There's a lot of pressure on the quarterback to know every play and execute it perfectly. In my son's early years of playing quarterback, he failed often. He would throw an interception and jog off the field in tears, feeling like a failure. Because I was a coach and on the sidelines, I would put my arm around him and tell him, "Forget about it. Go back out there and get us a touchdown." There's no time to sulk when you are the quarterback. You've got to lead your team. If you linger on your failures and believe you are helpless, you are sure to fail again. More than likely, you'll lose the game. Great quarterbacks know how to move on quickly from their very public failures.

You are the quarterback of your life. You've had your failures. You've jogged to the sidelines in tears. What will you do now? Will you linger and sulk in your failure assuring your next failure or will you get back in the game? The Apostle Paul understood the importance of forgetting the past and focusing on the future. He said this, "No, dear brothers, I am still not all I should be, but I am bringing all my energies to bear on this one thing: Forgetting the past and looking forward to what lies ahead, I strain to reach the end of the race and receive the prize for which God is calling us up to heaven. Because of what Christ Jesus did for us." Philippians 3:12-14, (The Living Bible)[2]

Paul wasn't perfect, and he knew it. But, he didn't let his failures keep him from moving forward. He focused all his energies on forgetting and moving forward. What if he sat around pouting about his failures? Perhaps the message of Jesus Christ would not have spread as quickly as it did through his missionary efforts and we definitely would not have the many letters he wrote that now serve as parts of the New Testament. Paul didn't believe his failures were fatal and neither should you. If you do, you lose and the world loses. Get back in the game.

QUESTIONS

1. Why is it important that you should not believe you are finished when you fail?

2. In what area of your life are you being tempted to quit and not get back in the game?

3. Who are the people that will be negatively impacted if you quit?

GOD'S VIEW OF FAILURE

You and God have a different perspective of failure. From His perspective, God can see everything. From your perspective, you can see very little. It's like watching a parade. Years ago, when the Atlanta Braves played in the World Series, everyone in Atlanta went crazy about the Braves and supported them even though they eventually lost the World Series. Even though they lost, everyone showed up for a huge parade through the streets of Atlanta.

I was only eighteen years old and ready for any adventure, so several friends and I headed down to watch the parade. We wanted to see the parade from the highest point so we made our way through the back alleys, rode elevators and climbed stairs to the highest point we could find. I remember watching the parade from that perspective. The famous players looked so small. The cars looked like toys, and the people looked like ants. We could see just about all the parade at once and take it all in. We watched the beginning, the middle and the end of the parade at the same time. It was interesting to watch as the entire parade moved like one unit.

Our perspective was much different from those who watched from the street. They were up close and personal. They were in the thick of the action, but they could only see one thing at a time. To them, the parade seemed like a series of cars and players passing by separately. But to us on the rooftops, it looked like one event.

God sees things from the perspective of the rooftop. He sees all of time at once. He sees the beginning, the middle and the end. He isn't surprised by anything. He's definitely not surprised by your failure. God has never said, "I didn't see that coming!" He knew you would fail before you failed. You might be surprised, but He isn't. God is not just everywhere, He's also everywhere in all time. When you finally showed up to your failure, God was already there. He wasn't surprised. When you are in the middle of your failure and it feels like your world is caving in around you, it's hard to see past your failure, but God has already seen past your failure and He's promised to work it for good.

> "God has already seen past your failure and He's promised to work it for good."

The Bible says, "And we know that in all things God works for the good of those who love him, who have been called according to his purpose." Romans 8:28 (NIV)[1]

The Apostle Paul understood God is working everything for your good. God always works your failures for your good. Paul didn't say God is just working the successes in your life for your good. God is working your failures, even your outright disobedience, for your good. The God who created everything by the power of His word and who holds all things together with the power of His word is completely capable of turning your failures into something good.

From your perspective, you probably can't see how anything

good can come from your failure. You can't see past your failure. But God does. You can't see the end, but God does. You can't understand how this can work for good, but God does. You can't understand His ways and His thoughts and you never will on this side of eternity. The Prophet Isaiah said this about God's thoughts and our thoughts, "For my thoughts are not your thoughts, neither are your ways my ways," declares the LORD. "As the heavens are higher than the earth, so are my ways higher than your ways and my thoughts than your thoughts. Isaiah 55:8,9 (NIV)[2]

I bet God laughs when we try to figure out His ways. His ways and His thoughts are too high for us to understand. We are at ground level while He's on the rooftops. We struggle to see how anything good can come from our failure, but we can be confident God is working our failure for our good. You have to believe you aren't finished, and God still has a plan for you even though you've failed. For those who will step back and trust God, there's a long parade full of twists and turns, but you can be sure—it's going to be good.

QUESTIONS

1. How does God's view of time differ from yours?
2. If God sees all of your life as one event, how do you think He views you?

CHANGE YOUR VIEW

The distraught young man sitting across from me at our local restaurant arranged to meet with me because he was struggling. I didn't know what he was struggling with, but I had a pretty good idea. I soon found out. It was the same thing most have struggled with —Porn.

Porn is destructive in so many ways and even those outside of religious communities are becoming aware of the damage porn does to women, men, families, marriages, and communities. Like a plague on our society, porn is wreaking havoc on our culture and eating away our moral fiber. I know because I've been there. I fought this battle in my own life, and I've felt its destructive power. The ease of access to porn makes it highly addictive and not too hard to hide. Its tentacles grip men and women from all walks of life in to a web of depression, hopelessness and despair. Almost weekly, I sit down and talk with men and women who are addicted to porn or whose lives are being torn apart by porn.

My young friend was another one of those who was broken over his sin and recent failure with porn. He's not the type of guy you would imagine would be struggling with porn. He genuinely loves Jesus and is one of the most passionate guys I know about his faith. He's the real deal. He longs to serve God with all his heart and plans to serve in ministry for the rest of his life. He was truly broken by his actions. He didn't want to look at porn. He knows what the Bible says about lust, and he has a heart that truly cares about protecting women. But he failed. He blew it, and you could see it on his face and hear it in his voice.

As we sat and ate, he looked over his yeast rolls the waitress brought us, and he shared his heart. He talked about how he hated himself for what he had done and was emotionally beating himself up. He was genuinely broken.

As he shared, my friend was taken back at my reaction to his confession. Instead of ridiculing him and making him feel like a loser for what he did, I helped him see his failure from a different point of view. He knew he had messed up and felt genuine remorse. The problem was that he didn't know how to respond to his failure. So often in churches, we're wrongly taught that extreme guilt and shame are the only adequate responses to our failures. My friend had those two emotions down well. He knew he was guilty and was ashamed of what he did. The problem was that he had never learned to look at his failure from another angle.

I wanted to help him see his failure from God's point of view. I asked him these two questions…

"How do you think God views you right now?"
"What good can come out of your failure?"

I asked him the first question because how he thinks God views him will determine his response to God. Very often, we have an inaccurate view of how God views us. I'll talk about this later on in the book. I asked him the second question because rarely do we see failure as something that can lead to something good. As we talked through the questions, the light bulb began to come on in his mind. He began to turn from the hopelessness and shame he first felt and he started finding hope and

"Until you see your failures from God's perspective, you'll never move forward."

purpose in his failure. People who live in hopelessness and shame eventually give up and never change. Those who find hope and purpose through their failure become the men and women God intends them to be.

Until you see your failures from God's perspective, you'll never move forward. I helped my friend see his failure from God's point of view and that failure does not equal finished. He left our lunch, hopeful and ready to learn what God wanted him to learn. I challenged him to ask God and himself what good does God want to bring out of his failure.

A few weeks later, we were talking again and he told me our lunch conversation had changed his life. He said he had only looked at failure one way in the past, but he had started to look at failure from God's perspective and that he was growing more than he had in a very long time. God wants the same for you. He wants you to move beyond your failure. Your failure does not equal finished. Until you see your failures from God's perspective, you'll continue to waste your failures and never move forward.

Before you move on to the next chapter, I encourage you to

stop and ask yourself the same questions I asked my friend. Ask God to help you to see your failure from His perspective and then think about these two questions at the end of this section. How you view your failure will determine your outcome. As you read further in this book ask God to expose any lies you've believed about your failure and to help you see your failure from His perspective.

QUESTIONS

1. How does God view me right now?
2. What good can come out of my failure?

CHAPTER 3

THE GOD OF FAILURES

"Failing is not a disgrace

unless you make it the last chapter of your book."

- Jack Hyles[1]

TWO FAILURES. TWO DIFFERENT OUTCOMES

Authenticity is rare, especially in the lives of religious people. You have to look hard to find genuinely authentic religious individuals who are open and honest about their failures. Too many church leaders and those who sit weekly in church services work too hard to cover their failures. I know. I'm one of them. There's a fear that we'll be exposed for who we really are. It's a shame because there's freedom in honesty and openness. It also helps others to live and learn from our mistakes. That's one of the reasons the Bible is so powerful. It doesn't hide the failures of even its greatest heroes. In the Bible, everyone's failures are all out in the open for everyone to see. It's also powerful because it gives us a very clear picture of how Jesus responds to our failures.

The story surrounding Jesus' betrayal is a powerful example of how Jesus responds to our failures. It's also a warning to us about how to react to our own failures. There were many people who made mistakes, failed or sinned when Jesus was arrested and crucified, but two of the most obvious failures were made by two of Jesus' closest friends. Judas and Peter were two men handpicked by Jesus to be a part of his inner crowd. For three years, the two men spent nearly every day with Jesus and the other ten disciples. They ate together, traveled together and served together. Peter and Judas watched Jesus perform many powerful miracles, and in some instances, they were a part of the miracles. They heard Him teach, saw Him behind the scenes and knew Him better than anyone. They were Jesus' closest friends, but in Jesus' most crucial moment, they failed Him.

There were two failures with two very different outcomes. The first four books of the New Testament describe how Judas betrayed Jesus by leading those who wanted to arrest Jesus to Him as He prayed. Upon his arrival in the garden, he identified Jesus by kissing Him on the cheek. Judas betrayed Jesus with a kiss! How low can you get? Plus, he betrayed Jesus for thirty pieces of silver! Judas failed. He failed big time. He betrayed a friend. He betrayed the miracle worker. He betrayed the Son of God. That may seem like a very isolated case of betrayal, but that night, every single one of Jesus' disciples would turn away from Jesus—including Peter.

Peter was a passionate man. He was quick to speak what was in his heart. His passion revealed itself through his mouth, and it was always getting him in trouble. He was one who was quick to boldly and loudly proclaim his love and support for Jesus. On the evening of Jesus's arrest, Peter boldly proclaimed, "even if all fall away on account of you, I never will." Matthew 26:33 (NIV)[1]

Jesus quickly stopped him and told Peter he would publicly deny him three times before the rooster crowed the next morning. Three different times that evening as Jesus stood on trial before his accusers, Peter denied he ever knew Jesus. At one point, he even called down curses on himself if he was lying about knowing Jesus. Then right as the rooster crowed for the third time, Jesus looked at Peter and he remembered Jesus' words. Peter failed. He failed big time. He broke his promise, and he denied ever knowing Jesus right in front of Him.

It's hard to imagine the guilt, shame and utter disappointment both men must have felt. Both men turned their back on the one who showed them nothing but love. The Bible says "When Judas, who had betrayed him, saw that Jesus was condemned, he was seized with remorse and returned the thirty pieces of silver to the chief priests and the elders." (Matthew 27:3 NIV)[2] Judas was eaten up with remorse. So much so that he wanted nothing to do with the money he received. Peter was also broken by his failure. After realizing he failed, Peter did what many of us do. He ran, he wept, and he believed he was finished.

Both men failed, and both men felt remorse, but their response to their failures was different. The Bible tells us that Satan entered Judas just before he betrayed Jesus. Somewhere in his thinking, he gave the enemy a crack and he took over. He gave into the enemy's lies and the enemy began working his plan to steal, kill and destroy. After his failure, Judas was eaten up with guilt and shame. While listening to Satan, Judas's remorse turned fatal. Judas walked out into a field, hung up a rope and hung himself from a limb. Eventually, the limb broke and his limp body fell to the ground as his bowels spilled out on the ground. Satan's scheme worked, and Judas was the victim. Judas believed his failure equaled finished. He could not see a future beyond his failure.

Peter, on the other hand, had a different response to his failure. Peter also blew it big time. He knew he messed up and he broke a promise he had just made. Worst of all, he betrayed Jesus three times to his face. Even though he messed up terribly, Peter was broken by his failure and eaten up with remorse. He didn't believe the enemy's lies. He didn't believe his failure equal finished. He went back to the other disciples, but something was different. He was humbled.

In his humility, Peter had hope. He returned to fishing and waited. He waited to see what would happen and if God could still use him. After his resurrection, Jesus sought Peter out and found him fishing. When Jesus called out to him from the shore, Peter didn't run and hide. He didn't sit in fear. He wildly jumped in the water with both feet and quickly made his way to Jesus. Jesus sought out His betrayer, and He didn't condemn him. He didn't scold him. He didn't even tell him how disappointed He was. No. Jesus made breakfast and ate with him. Then a beautiful picture of grace unfolded. Jesus restored him to ministry. He failed, but he wasn't finished.

"God invites you to trade your guilt for grace."

Like Peter and Judas, we all fail. We break promises and give in to temptations. We fail to reach our goals or fail to do the right thing, but when we fail, we have a choice. You can choose the outcome. You can go the way of Judas or you can go the way of Peter. One leads to death; the other leads to life. The temptation is to make an agreement with the enemy and believe you are finished. If you choose that path, it will drive you down a dark path of hopelessness and despair. But if you chose to take the path of Peter, it leads to a future better than your past.

God wants you to see beyond your failure and start experiencing His grace. God invites you to trade your guilt for grace. His grace encourages you to keep going and to have hope.

Your guilt wants you to give up. There's a constant battle that wars in us when we fail. Guilt shouts, "You are worthless and finished." Grace quietly whispers, "You're not finished." You can live in guilt or you live in grace. The choice is yours.

QUESTIONS

1. What do you think was going on inside the minds of Peter and Judas after they failed?

2. Do you find yourself thinking more like Peter or Judas? What will that kind of thinking lead to in your life? Will it get you the outcome you desire?

3. Why did Jesus seek out Peter after he failed? Could Jesus also be seeking you?

JESUS LOVES FAILURES

Recently, a longtime friend and ministry partner blessed me with a sword that had unexpected meaning and value to me. I'm not a collector of swords or one of those people wishing they lived in the Medieval times. I like electricity, the Internet and deodorant. The sword was a gift from my friend, Trent Dollyhigh, representing my leadership in our church starting a second campus. That same church campus became our first new church plant.

Trent was the Pastor for our second campus and we worked together for eight years side-by-side in ministry until we launched the campus into a new church. Trent surprised me one Sunday morning at the end of our church service when he unexpectedly came over from his new church plant and appeared on our stage with a huge shiny sword. I had no idea what he was doing. My first thought was "Who just lets a guy walk onto a stage with a sword in a church service?" Quickly, I found out why he was there. Trent honored me and thanked me in front of my congregation for believing in him and investing my life in planting the new church. He even awkwardly "knighted" me in front of my congregation and presented me with the sword. It was a very meaningful and special event. Plus, I got a really cool sword as a memorial of what God did through my life.

The next day, I placed the sword in my office and carefully admired it. The sword is engraved with intricate detail and looks like it's made for a king. As I was appreciating the sword, I noticed a large chip in the handle. My first thought was, "Why would he give me a chipped sword? Don't I deserve a perfect one?" Then as I examined the chip, it struck me that the chipped sword is perfect. I was reminded, "I'm not a perfect leader and I don't serve a perfect church."

The chipped sword represents my church and me perfectly.

"We value the pretty and the perfect. Jesus values the chipped and broken."

On the large windows above the main entrance of our church there's a saying in massive print. It says, "Welcome to the perfect church for people who aren't." I believe that sword was chipped on purpose to remind me that there are no perfect people, no perfect leaders, and no perfect churches. All churches are full of chipped people. A few days later, I spoke with Trent and he asked if I noticed the chip in the sword. He mentioned that after he ordered the sword and it came to his house, he noticed it was chipped. Then he came to the same conclusion I did. The sword is perfect as it is. The chipped sword represents my church and me perfectly. We're all chipped and no one knows it better than pastors.

The chip in the sword reminds me Jesus values things we reject. We value the pretty and the perfect, but Jesus values the chipped and broken. We value the perfect diamond or the perfect car. We admire the perfect game or the perfect body. Jesus values the imperfect, the chipped and the broken. All throughout Jesus' ministry, He sought out broken people and He despised people who thought they were perfect. He was constantly spending time with the outcast, broken and chipped. Yet, He had nothing but scorn for the religious leaders who couldn't see the chips in their own armor. On one occasion, Jesus addressed the religious leaders who were emphasizing perfect living but who couldn't see their own imperfections. He said to them, "Woe to you, teachers of the law and Pharisees, you hypocrites! You are like whitewashed tombs, which look beautiful on the outside but on the inside are full of the bones of the dead and everything unclean. In the same way, on the outside you appear to people as righteous but on the inside you are full of hypocrisy and wickedness." Matt 23:27, 28 (NIV)[1]

Jesus looked beyond the outer appearance of the religious leaders who looked like they lived perfect lives. He called them out and rebuked them for covering their failures. He knew that underneath their religious disguise, they were just as broken as the rest of us. Jesus despises those who try to cover their failure, but values those who are broken by their failure.

Jesus gave tremendous value to the people who failed. He sought after a woman at a well who had five different husbands and who was living with another man. He didn't avoid her or condemn her. He sought her out, valued her and gave her hope. On another occasion, Jesus pursued the greediest and most despised man in town. He found the ruthless and greedy tax collector, Zacchaeus, in a tree and invited Himself over for dinner. Zacchaeus was radically changed by Jesus' love and acceptance. Later, He stepped in front of an angry crowd as they attempted to stone a woman for adultery. He valued her enough to put Himself in the path of hurled rocks. He sought each of them out because Jesus values broken people.

It amazes me that the God of perfection values and pursues imperfect people. It seems that a perfect and Holy God would pursue perfect people but He does the opposite of what we think. Jesus pursues failures. If you've failed, Jesus is pursuing you. When you fail, it's easy to believe you're finished, but Jesus doesn't cast you to the side and discard you. He pursues you,

"Jesus doesn't wait till you're perfect to love you."

He finds you and He delivers you from your regrets. It's hard for us to believe God still wants chipped people. We quickly discard broken products and broken people, but Jesus has vast love for broken people. Romans 5:8 says, "But God shows his love for us in that while we were still sinners, Christ died for us." (NIV)[2] It doesn't say Christ died for perfect people. It says Christ died for people who were imperfect.

Jesus doesn't wait till you're perfect to love you. He loves you in your imperfection. Jesus still loves you and wants you. You're still the one He is pursuing. However, there's a problem. Your imperfection keeps you from having a relationship with God. God is perfect and can have nothing to do with sin. Unless you've been forgiven by God for the things you've done wrong, there's a relational gap between you and God. Though we all have sinned, that hasn't kept God from pursuing us and making a way for us to be close to Him. The Bible says, "God made him who had no sin to be sin for us, so that in him we might become the righteousness of God." 2 Cor 5:21 (NIV)[3]

The Bible teaches that God sent His son, Jesus, from Heaven to Earth to live among us. Jesus lived as we live but He was perfect. He never sinned. Jesus never failed. Because He never failed, He was able to die on a cross in your place as a sacrifice for your imperfections and remove the punishment you deserve.

There's only one way the gap between you and God can be restored. You must confess to God that you have sinned and trust that Jesus died for you. The Bible says, "Yet to all who did receive him, to those who believed in his name, he gave the right to become children of God." John 1:12 (NIV)[4]

If you receive what Jesus did for you, then you can become a cherished child of God. The big question is, "Have you ever trusted in Jesus and been forgiven?" If no, you can do it right now. Before you read another paragraph, stop and confess to God that you have failed miserably in your life and that you believe Jesus died for you. You can do it right where you are. God will hear you and find you. He still wants you. He still pursues you. Will you let Him restore you?

If you are already a Christian, you may believe your failure equals finished. You may be eaten up with guilt, shame or remorse. You need to know your failure hasn't decreased your value to Jesus. You are still loved, still pursued and still valuable to God. You're chipped but God values chipped people. Do you believe that? Do you believe it with more than just your mind? Do you feel it deep down in your heart? Do you feel it at your core that Jesus loves you and wants you? Until you do, you'll have a hard time moving beyond your failure. If you want to move on from your failure, it's important that you believe God loves you and wants you. It's time to start believing it. Repeat out loud after me. "Jesus loves me and wants me." Say it again. Now, say it like you mean it. "Jesus loves me and wants me!" Say it again and again until you believe it.

QUESTIONS

1. Why do you think God pursues imperfect people?
2. What reasons do you give for why God shouldn't love you?
3. Do those reasons line up with the Jesus we see in scripture?

IN GOOD COMPANY

When I was young, I believed Pastors were perfect. I would listen to their powerful sermons and they moved my soul. I was amazed at their ability to preach so powerfully. I would look at the lives they portrayed on a stage and believe they must never fail. I would imagine that they never gave into lust, got up too late or lost their temper. I imagined they had perfectly managed lives and that God was really pleased with them. That led me to believe the source of their amazing preaching ability was their sinless lives.

Why did I believe that? I believed that because you rarely ever heard a Pastor talk about his failures. Sure, they talked about when they got a speeding ticket or had occasional argument with their wife, but it seemed like they never failed. They never seemed to talk about real failures, especially like the ones I could relate to.

I would constantly stay frustrated with my inability to live perfectly like the guys on the stage. I would make promises, cry, scream and even get people to hold me accountable in my attempts to live a perfect Christian life. It seemed like I was on a constant cycle of sin-confess-repeat.

When I was a teen, every time I would go to Summer Camp, I would be convinced that I failed so much during the rest of the year that I must not really be a Christian. I would decide I needed to become a "real" Christian and get baptized again. I think I got baptized four times as a teenager! Like most teenagers in their formative years, failure was a daily occurrence. I think it was probably more like an hourly occurrence for me.

I remember many well-meaning but scary sermons about living a Holy life and making sure you are 100% confident you are a Christian because eternity was too long to be wrong. Those things are true, but I wish I would have heard more teaching about the God of Failures.

You see, when I read the Bible, I read very few stories about perfect leaders or preachers. There is an overwhelming number of stories about "Failures" that God still used. There are many more of those kinds than there are stories about people who got it right.

When you read the Bible, it's easy to see there are no perfect people or perfect heroes. Everyone has their flaws and everyone fails. The only real hero is Jesus. Everyone else needs His grace. I wish I had learned more about walking in grace and coming back from failure than I did about starting all over again. I wish I would have learned that failure doesn't equal finished. Instead, I believed God only used perfect people.

We often fall into the trap of believing that God only uses perfect people. We think He wouldn't use someone like us who gives up too quickly, fails to keep commitments or lets their laziness get the best of them. He surely can't use people who have an addiction, can't control their temper or live in fear. What about individuals who've failed so many times they've lost count of their failures? God can't use people like that, can He?

You should know His answer by now. The answer is—Yes! God can still use you! He's not finished with you. Your failure does not equal finished.

The story of Peter is not the only story in the Bible about God using someone who failed to do great things. All through the Old Testament and New Testament, there are stories of men and women that had big failures, small failures and multiple failures but God was not finished with them.

Abraham was one of those notable failures. If you know the story of Abraham, you are probably familiar with the incredible faith he had to offer his son to God as a sacrifice. If you don't know the story, don't get freaked out. He didn't kill his son, but he had faith that God would provide an alternate sacrifice. But, before Abraham was a great man of faith, he failed miserably when he had to trust God. Twice, he lied and said his wife was his sister and let her live with another man so that he wouldn't be killed. He put his wife and the promise of God at risk because he didn't trust God.

On another occasion, God promised Abraham he would have a son even though his wife was barren. When the baby didn't come, Abraham took things into his own hands rather than trusting God. He slept with his maid and she had a son. This act caused tremendous pain and hardship for many, including Abraham. But, God didn't write Abraham off. Eventually, Abraham learned from his failures and learned to have unwavering faith in God. When it seemed impossible, Abraham's wife had a son.

Abraham wasn't perfect, but that didn't mean God was finished with him. His failures did not limit God's plans and as we will see in the next chapter, Abraham's failures were working for his good.

Abraham wasn't the only Old Testament figure to fail. Moses was a major failure also. You may know that Moses was used by God to rescue his people out of slavery in Egypt. He performed many miracles, led the people through the desert and even received the Ten Commandments from God Himself. At one point, he was so close to the presence of God that the Bible says his face literally glowed after he came down a mountain after being in God's presence.

Moses is a hero of the Christian faith, but he's also a failure. Before he became the leader that God would use to rescue his people, Moses was a murderer on the run. He killed a man in Egypt and tried to cover it up. When he found out that people knew he committed the murder, he took off and hid out in the desert for forty years. Moses failed big time! He murdered a man and never paid the penalty. In our modern day, he'd be one of the faces you see in the news that is wanted for murder. He might even have been on the most wanted list.

> "God doesn't use perfect people. God uses broken people who've been refined by failure."

Moses was a murderer and an outlaw, but God wasn't finished with him. In time, God redeemed Moses and turned an outlaw into a humble leader. Moses eventually learned from his failure, and he let it shape him into a man of God.

Don't be fooled. There are no perfect people and no one has it all together. God doesn't use perfect people. God uses broken people who've been refined by failure. If you've failed, you are in good company. You are in the company of Peter, Abraham, Moses and many other people in the Bible who blew it.

Maybe you've haven't failed as bad as Peter, Abraham or Moses. Maybe your failure is smaller and doesn't seem as serious. It may be smaller, but if it's keeping you from moving forward and experiencing the life that God intends for you, then it's a failure that's gotten too big. The good news is that if God wasn't finished with those guys, he's not finished with you. The God of Failures is able to turn your situation into something good, and in the next chapter, we'll discover what that means.

QUESTIONS

1. Why do you think God often uses people who have failed to do great things?
2. Take a minute and imagine how God could still use you in the future.

CHAPTER 4

GOOD FROM BAD

"We failed, but in the good providence of God

apparent failure often proves a blessing."

- Assorted Authors[1]

NOTHING LEFT TO TRY

In May 2013, I hit rock bottom. I was at the lowest point of my life. I was ready to walk away from seventeen years of ministry, my church and my calling. I was unhealthy, anxious and depressed. I couldn't sleep, but I also didn't want to get out of bed. I was a mess.

I felt insignificant and worthless. Negative thoughts polluted my mind daily. I was uselessly medicating my depression with food and other destructive behaviors. I didn't want to go to work or be around anyone. My friendships were fracturing. My ministry was suffering. My life was one big joyless, monotonous Merry-Go-Round.

My relationship with God was as stale as week old french-fries. There was nothing there. It seemed as if I was a million miles away from God. Praying was a chore. Teaching was chore. Serving others was a chore. That's difficult if you're paid to be the "professional" Christian. One of the most gut-wrenching things to do is speak before a crowd of people who are desperate to hear from God when you haven't seriously talked to Him in months. There were times when I honestly thought about just not showing up to preach. When I went home on Sundays, I would literally moan and just lay in my bed because I felt like such a hypocrite.

Heaven sounded better to me each day. I even envied those who passed away because the struggle for them was over. They ran their race, and now they were no longer struggling in this hard world. I was tired of struggling and tired of failing. I felt like a failure every day.

What got me to such a low, desperate place? Why did I feel like a failure? I felt like a failure because I was failing to be the man I believed I should be. When I observed my life, I could see I was failing in every area. I was failing in my ministry, my marriage, my health, my friendships, my finances and my relationship with God. Everywhere I looked, I saw unmet dreams and goals. I believed I should be further along in my ministry, financially stable, well-liked, important, free from lust, healthy and intimate with God. I couldn't be the man I wanted to be. I believed I should be more. I failed every day I breathed. I believed I was failing God, the people around me and myself.

I was convinced God was disappointed with me. I imagined he was constantly shaking his head in complete disappointment at my efforts to be a Christian man. Talking to him was not something I felt I could do. Instead, I kept my distance and my life grew darker.

I knew things had to change. At a monthly meeting with the Elders of my church, I finally shared my desperate situation with the men around the table. They sat and listened with concern and compassion. I then asked for time away from my duties as a Pastor. I asked for a four-week sabbatical so I could get my bearings. They generously agreed and allowed me to take it as soon as I was able to work out the details of my absence. Four weeks later, I walked out of the office unsure if I would return.

I wasn't sure what to do with my time. I read a few books about what to do during a sabbatical, and I talked with few friends who gave me some advice. I didn't know what to do or how to use my time. I just knew I didn't want to fail at this too. I decided I would just focus on getting closer to God even though I was sure He was disappointed in me.

That dark season turned into one of the greatest seasons of growth for me. I had no idea what God was going to do and the things He would teach me. He used that dark season to develop His image in me.

As I searched for answers and attempted to grow closer to him, I picked up a few books to read. I wasn't even sure what to read, but God knew what he wanted me to hear. I was a defeated and beat up Pastor looking for a reason to keep believing and to get back in the game. Daily, I would just read, nap and read some more. The whole time, I was looking for the thing God wanted me to learn.

I promised to take my daughter on a mission trip to the Dominican Republic that summer and I wasn't going to back out on her. In the middle of my sabbatical, we headed to the Dominican Republic. I sent her out with the team most days and they would allow me to stay back and just read. It was there on a blow-up mattress, with one hundred and ten-degree heat and a fan blowing on high two feet from my face that God spoke to me. His message changed the whole way I viewed my life.

As I read the books, a theme emerged and it hit me like a ton of bricks. The theme was grace. Grace was something I knew about. I taught on it many times. You can't be an evangelical Pastor and not know about grace. I knew about grace, but grace was something I never fully grasped for myself and didn't even know I needed until that moment. I was failing in every area of

my life and feeling like God was finished with me when I read
this sentence...

> "because Jesus was strong for me,
> I was free to be weak;
> because Jesus won for me,
> I was free to lose;
> because Jesus was someone,
> I was free to be no one;
> because Jesus was extraordinary,
> I was free to be ordinary;
> because Jesus succeeded for me,
> I was free to fail."[1]

That one sentence changed my perspective on everything. It
was then that God showed me I'm free to fail because Jesus
succeeded for me. I don't have to succeed. I don't have to win. I
don't have to be someone special. Jesus was already those things
for me! Bam! The thought that Jesus was already perfect for me
blew me away. I was moved in the core of my being. I was
finally starting to understand grace and find the beauty in my
failure. Look at what this verse says about how God has
succeeded for us, "the Father ...qualified you to share in the
inheritance of his holy people in the kingdom of light." Col 1:12
(NIV)[2]

We are qualified already through Jesus! We don't need
anything else to win God's approval. Jesus won the Father's
approval for us. For an attention-seeking, weak, fame hungry,

failing Pastor, those words were like a warm meal to a starving beggar. I was failing at everything but it was okay. Jesus succeeded for me!

God had a purpose for my failure. Failure taught me the most important lesson—God's grace is enough. Grace changed from something I just knew about to something I experienced. Until I fully realized my own lack of ability to be good enough, I couldn't fully embrace God's amazing grace for me.

> **"I don't have to succeed. I don't have to win. I don't have to be someone special. Jesus was already those things for me!"**

Failure has an important purpose. Failure reveals your need for Grace. I couldn't experience and appreciate grace until I failed. I couldn't be free until I failed. Grace wasn't amazing for me until I reached the bottom.

You may be wondering why you're going through this dark season of failure. God wants to give you something. He wants to give you what you can't earn and what you don't expect. He offers you His favor and love simply because He wants to. He wants you to experience His amazing grace and love. As my friend Jason Glaze says, "Only failures are ready for grace. Everyone else has one more thing to try."

QUESTIONS

1.   What do you think is the greatest thing God wants to give

you through your failure?

2. If God qualified you to share in His inheritance and His grace which is sufficient, why do you think you still aren't enough?

GETTING WHAT YOU DO NOT DESERVE

Failure is a difficult teacher but it's good at its job. There are valuable lessons that can only be learned through the hardship of failure. My Dad and cars taught me a lot about failure, and through them, I learned even more about the beauty of forgiveness. When I was a teen, I was hard on cars, but I was blessed to have a father that worked on cars for a living. He regularly came across affordable cars, and he purchased my first. Like most Dads, I don't he think he knew what he was getting himself into when he purchased a car for me. He spent much of his time, after I started driving, taking care of the cars I damaged.

I'll never forget my first car. It was a 1979 Buick Regal. My friends and I named it the "Raging Regal." The car wasn't much to look at. It was the color of a penny and as long as a yacht. It was supposed to seat five people, but once, I managed to fit thirteen friends inside it. The car was ten years old and wasn't exactly the car a sixteen-year-old dreams of driving. But, I didn't mind. It was my car, and I was proud to have some wheels!

I drove the Raging Regal hard. In the first year, the car needed a new engine and lots of other work. Each time the car needed work, my Dad wouldn't just fix it for free. He would make sure I knew how much it was going to cost and then he would tell me I would have to repay him the money. The money I owed my Dad quickly began to accumulate. Within two years, I owed my Dad more than the car's worth.

After two years of driving the Buick and doing constant repairs, my Dad sold the car and bought me another one. The deal was that I would have to repay the old debt and pay for the new car also. The debt I owed my Dad continued to increase. You would think I would have learned my lesson about taking care of cars, but like lots of teens, I thought money just grew on trees.

I was hard on my new car also. On one occasion while trying to show off for some girls, one of whom was my Pastor's daughter, I wrecked my car into the large cement water drain in front of my Pastor's house. I had to leave it there overnight and have it towed the next day. The drain was damaged and looked awful. Needless to say, my Pastor, Dr. Johnny Hunt, wasn't very happy with me. He made sure to let me know the next day at church.

My Dad was livid. The car should have been totaled, but he knew people who could fix it. It would cost me again. It was another debt on top of the already massive debt I owed my Dad. By the time I was ready to graduate, I owed my Dad more money than I could possibly repay him.

I lived with the constant guilt of owing my Dad money. I made many failed attempts to repay him, but the debt seemed to never go away. Debt is awful. It is a constant source of irritation and guilt. We've probably all experienced it. It hangs over us regularly and makes us a slave. I hated the debt and didn't want to graduate in debt and at odds with my Dad. That's when my dad taught me one of my greatest lessons about failure and forgiveness.

The day of my graduation from high school, we had a big celebration at our home. Friends and family came together at our home to eat and congratulate me for graduating. Many of them brought gifts and cards. I loved the cards because they were full of money. I saved my parents card for last. When I opened the card, I expected a check or some money to fall out.

> "Forgiveness is God resetting your account from negative to zero. Grace is God adding to your account more than you could ever repay."

There was some money inside, but it was what was written inside the card that impacted me the most. Inside the card was encouraging and loving words from my parents, but there was one phrase from my Dad I still remember. It was this; "I want you to start the next season of your life fresh. The debt you owe me is forgiven. You owe me nothing." I still remember the feeling of relief I felt that moment. I remember looking at my Dad in shock and profusely thanking him. I felt free, relieved and blessed. My Dad released me from my debt and I could start fresh without the nagging feeling of constantly owing him money. I'll never forget that moment. Complete and total forgiveness is unforgettable.

That one event taught me so much about forgiveness. The word forgive literally means "to grant relief from payment of."[1] My Dad relieved me of the payment I owed him. In the process, he let me go free of the guilt I constantly felt. The Heavenly

Father forgives us the same way. When He forgives us of our debts, sins and disobedience, He completely releases us from owing Him anything. He let it go. It's a wonderful feeling to know that you owe God nothing. He releases us from our failures and we are set free. God's forgiveness is more than enough, but He goes another step.

God gives us more than forgiveness. He gives us grace. Grace is a step beyond forgiveness. It does what forgiveness can't. Forgiveness is God letting go of the thing you owe Him, but grace is God giving you what you do not deserve. Forgiveness is God resetting your account from negative to zero. Grace is God adding to your account more than you could ever repay. Forgiveness is God removing His condemnation from you. Grace is God showing you His favor and giving you what you don't deserve. Here's how I like to define grace…

"Grace is the undeserved love and favor
God gives to people just because he wants to."

God doesn't have to show us grace, but He wants to. He loves giving people what they least expect and what they can never earn. It's completely opposite of how we often treat people. We tend to give people only what they deserve and what they expect. If someone mistreats us, we often do the same to him or her. God does the opposite. He gives what is not expected or deserved. He shows kindness and showers us with blessings.

I believe one the greatest lessons that failure teaches us is the lesson about grace. Without failure, we have a super-human complex or mini-god syndrome that makes us think we can do anything without God's help. Failure has a way of bringing us to our knees and reminding us of our brokenness.

The funny thing about grace is that it takes on two forms. Dietrich Bonhoeffer describes the two forms of grace as "Cheap Grace" and "Costly Grace." He describes cheap grace as something that we may know in our minds, but the cost of the grace is never really felt or appreciated. Costly grace is grace that changes a person. In his book, "The Cost of Discipleship," Bonhoeffer describes costly grace like this,

> "Costly grace is the gospel which must be sought again and again and again, the gift which must be asked for, the door at which a man must knock. Such grace is costly because it calls us to follow, and it is grace because it calls us to follow Jesus Christ. It is costly because it costs a man his life, and it is grace because it gives a man the only true life. It is costly because it condemns sin, and grace because it justifies the sinner. Above all, it is costly because it cost God the life of his Son: 'Ye were bought at a price', and what has cost God much cannot be cheap for us. Above all, it is grace because God did not reckon his Son too dear a price to pay for our life, but delivered him up for us. Costly grace is the Incarnation of God."[2]

Complete and utter failure has a way of teaching us about costly grace. It reminds us of our inability to save ourselves and our great need for God's amazing grace. Failure reconciled by the healing balm of costly grace changes you forever.

Jesus loves to encounter failure with grace, and it was the

costly grace that transformed Peter. After Peter denied Jesus and Jesus was crucified, John 21 tells us that Peter and the other disciples went back to what they were doing before they ever met Jesus. Peter was a fisherman, so he returned to fishing. You can imagine what was going through his mind. There's no doubt he believed he was finished. He assumed he would never be useful to God again and Jesus was finished with him. He had seen Jesus after His resurrection but wasn't convinced he would ever be allowed to serve him again. Peter believed his failure equaled finished.

Sometime later, Jesus approached the disciples at sunrise and called to them from the shoreline as the men were fishing from a boat. He asked for some fish, but they had caught none. Jesus then tells them where to cast their nets and after doing so, they caught 153 fish. The disciples immediately recognized the stranger on the shore as Jesus. Peter awkwardly and passionately leaped into the water as he made his way to the shore to see Jesus. He longed to see Jesus again after His resurrection, but you can sense the tension in the relationship. Peter wants to be accepted, but knows he's failed. As Peter approached the shore, he found that Jesus had already started a fire and he invites Peter to breakfast.

Who does that? Who invites a betrayer to have breakfast? Who seeks out the person who hurt you, fixes them breakfast and invites them to sit down and talk? No one I know does that. No one blesses a betrayer. Nevertheless, Jesus does. He prepares him a meal and then sits down to share it with him.

During the conversation, Jesus didn't rebuke or scold Peter. He just asks Peter three times if he still loves him. Peter humbly answers, "Yes, you know I love you." Jesus responds each time: "Feed my sheep." That phrase is an invitation from Jesus to get back in the game and serve him by serving others. Jesus didn't remind him of his failure. He revealed his future. Peter fully expected to be told he was finished, but Jesus gave him what he was not expecting and cannot earn. He gave him grace. He was restored and given a place of prominence among the disciples.

We have a hard time imagining that broken things can be of value again, so we quickly discard broken things. If something breaks, we throw it away. We have mountains of discarded trash covered over with dirt in landfills in every community. In every community, there are also many people who are broken and cast aside. They've failed in many ways and they feel hopeless. They feel like discarded trash. Jesus seeks out the broken in every community and shows them grace. He restores them and gives them a future.

"With God, you don't always get what you deserve. He loves to give what is unexpected and underserved."

With God, you don't always get what you deserve. He loves to give what is unexpected and underserved. If you've failed, Jesus wants to restore you. You aren't finished. He has a future for you.

You may think you deserve to suffer, be punished or never to have success. You may feel like Peter who turned his back on

Jesus and wondered if God still has a plan and purpose for your life. You might wonder if your life will ever have any true significance because you keep failing. Whatever you're feeling or believing, you need to know—with Jesus, failure does not equal finished. Jesus restores the broken and He will restore you. You don't have to be perfect. Jesus was perfect already. You don't have to be a success. Jesus was a success already for you. You can rest in His success and grace.

Yes, you've failed, but you're not finished. Failure has a lesson to teach you before you move on. Perhaps God wants to teach you about His amazing grace. Before you rush on, take the time to ask God what He wants you to learn about Him through your failure. It may be that God desires to give you what you don't deserve and what you don't expect. He may go the extra step and bless you just like He did Peter. He offers you a future beyond your failure.

QUESTIONS

1. What is the difference between forgiveness and grace?
2. What do you think you deserve for your failure?
3. What could your life look like if God were to give you what you don't deserve and what you don't expect?

THE DARKROOM

There's a growing interest among young adults who were born after the invention of the digital camera. They are quickly finding an interest in developing their own film in a dark room. In the rush to have instant photography and to see the image we just shot with our camera, we've left behind a tedious but beautiful process of watching an anticipated image appear before our eyes in a dark room.

There's something wonderful about snapping a photo and then working with your hands to develop your own picture. I know because I spent some time in a dark room in college at North Greenville University where I studied Fine Arts and Religion. I remember the hours spent attempting to shoot the perfect picture and not knowing if I actually captured the image I wanted. After taking the picture I had to take special care of the film so that I didn't expose it to light. After that, I removed the film in a dark room that was lit only by a small red bulb. The film was then transferred onto photo paper and then carefully submerged into the right mix of photography chemicals. After placing the image in the pan, I swirled the chemicals over the paper until the magical moment happened. Then, after a few moments and all the hard work, the long awaited image would appear and I would discover if the next Ansell Adams was born. Processing film in a dark room is a lot of hard work for just one picture. It takes lots of time and resources to simply see one image.

Failure is much like the process of developing film in a dark room. Just as an image on film must go through the tedious and costly process of a dark room for its image to be exposed, God allows us to go through the darkness of failure to bring out his image in us. God knows what he wants to make of you and he's using your failures to develop his image in you. God has a purpose for your failure. Failure is one of the means by which God reveals his image in you. You might only become the person God wants you to become because of the failure you are facing today. Have you ever considered that the thing God wants you to learn might only be learned through today's disappointment?

Failure is often so unpleasant we want to quickly move on, but doing so hinders the process of what God desires to do in us. When we fail we want to hurry through our "darkroom," but just like developing film, you can't rush the process or you won't get the right image. If you remove the image from the chemical bath too soon, your photo will not fully develop and you'll be left with an image that lacks depth and beauty.

You're in the dark room for a reason. God wants to develop something in you. It's something beautiful and eternal. The Bible says, "For our light and momentary troubles are achieving for us an eternal glory that far outweighs them all." 2 Cor 4:17 (NIV)[1]

Notice the many powerful things this verse says about your troubles. First it says - Your troubles are momentary. Your failure won't last forever. When you are in the dark room it can seem you'll never see the light of day again. But, just as the photograph is only in the dark room for a short period, you too are only in this dark period for a short season. There is an end and there will be a day when you look back and think, "That went by faster than I imagined." Remember, God is working to develop something in you and when it is complete the season will be over. Are you having a hard time seeing a future beyond your failure? It may be because you you've believed this dark season is going to last forever. Hear this... "It won't last forever." God has promised your trouble is momentary. This season will pass and if you join with God in what he's wanting to do in your life, you'll be better in the end. Decide to believe, "This won't last forever."

> **"When we fail we want to hurry through our 'darkroom,' but just like developing film, you can't rush the process or you won't get the right image."**

It also says - Your failures are accomplishing something for you. When we experience failure we think we are taking a step back but God has a different view. God sees a setback as a setup for comeback. The verse says that God is accomplishing something for YOU. Hear that again - God has something for YOU. It's something that can only be learned through the difficulty and pain of failure. It's something you will never have unless you fail. Instead of viewing your troubles as a setback, start to view them as God wanting to accomplish something for you.

Sometimes failure is the very thing God desires for you. Read that again. Let that soak in. SOMETIMES FAILURE IS THE

VERY THING GOD DESIRES FOR YOU. That's hard for us to imagine in our world of Name-It-Claim-It Theology.[2] It's as if God is the kind, rich, white-bearded Grandpa in the sky waiting to give us the gifts we desire. That type of thinking says - if you pray the right way, have enough faith and do the right things, then God will give you what you want. It has left many people broken and feeling hopeless when their efforts were not met with success.

There's a common lie that says, "God wants to give you success." At the root of that lie is the belief, "If God is for me, I will be successful." The problem is in the way we define success. God's definition of success and our definition of success don't always match up.

"True success is the development of God's character and glory in you."

Success in God's book isn't you achieving your goals, dreams and agendas. True success is the development of God's character and glory in you. He desires to see you become more like him in your thoughts, words and actions. Failure is a great developer of character. You can be sure God will use the darkness of your failure to develop his character and glory in you.

How has God used failure in your past for your good? If you look hard enough, you'll see God hasn't wasted your past failures. He also won't waste your current failure. He's achieving something eternal in you.

The verse also reminds us – The growth God is doing

through your failure far outweighs your current discomfort. The darkness is never pleasant but it has a purpose. God is developing something greater in you. In most of our lives we can look back and see that our greatest growth usually came as a result of failure. It's through failure that God usually teaches us the most about ourselves and about him. We make a mistake when we believe God is only at work in our lives when we have success. He is also just as much at work when we experience failure. Barbara Duguid emphasizes this in her book *Extravagant Grace: God's Glory Displayed in our Weakness.* She says, "It is a radical and almost frightening thought to see that God is actually as much at work in our worst moments of sin and defeat as he is in our best moments of shining obedience."[3] The work God is doing in you through your failure will be greater than the pain, fear and doubt you are experiencing.

If failure ultimately works for our good, should we then attempt to fail on purpose? No! The "darkroom" process of learning through failure takes patience and is never easy. It would be best if we just learned the lesson God wants us to learn without all the pain, but sometimes the only way we'll get it is if God takes us through the darkness. That means we should strain toward becoming more like him in our thoughts and action every day. If we fail, we can be sure God will still use it for our good.

Your failure has purpose and God is developing something in you. In our success and performance driven culture it's hard to understand that failure may be the thing God desires for you. He is working and he's taking his time to get the perfect image. If you want to see the end result of your growth, then don't waste your pain. Slow down. Sit a while in the dark room and start to develop. Start by asking God some questions. Start with these…

QUESTIONS

1. God, why am I going through this failure?
2. God, how are you using this failure for my good?
3. God, what do you want to say to me about my failure?

THE POTTER'S WHEEL

There's something beautiful about watching a potter form the soft, damp clay spinning on his potter's wheel. An experienced potter can form the lump of formless clay into something useful and beautiful. A potter can shape it into the perfect coffee cup that will bring enjoyment to its owner or an intricate vase that sits on a mantle. The potter can easily form the spinning clay with just the light touch of a finger or thumb. The clay does whatever the potter forces it to do. Each lump of clay has the same potential and can become whatever the potter intends for it to become if the clay is suitable for use.

I had the opportunity to work with clay in college. I took several pottery classes and also had the chance to spend the summer assisting my professor, Professor Craft, with a pottery show that he was preparing. I enjoyed taking each lump of clay and spinning it through my hands to form useful and beautiful objects, then creating glazes that made each creation unique. I still have some of my creations in my house today.

I'll never forget the lesson Professor Craft taught me as we sat at the potter's wheel together one summer. As we talked, he took a lump of clay and placed it on the wheel. Then he took a small rock and pushed it with his thumb into the center of the clay. He covered the rock with the clay, wet his hands and started spinning the clay on the wheel. As the clay spun on the wheel, he pushed the clay up and down with his hand. The clay looked like every other lump we had molded with our hands.

He pushed down into the center of the clay as it spun and then pinched it outward as it formed a bowl. Next, he pinched the sides of the bowl and forced the clay upwards as it began to form a large vase.

The once formless lump of clay was taking on a purposeful and attractive shape. It was growing taller and the walls were getting thinner as he used both hands to form the vase. As the vase spun on the wheel, it looked like every other vase we had created until the walls got thin enough and a lump formed on one of the sides of the vase. The rock that was invisible in the clay at the beginning was now starting to show up. Then, right as the vase was reaching its maximum height, the vase came violently tumbling and crashing back down to its base. The beautiful vase was a mess. It lay crumbled and torn on the wheel with parts of it hanging off the edge. He took his hand and traced the tear in the clay all the way back to its beginning. It was there at the tear the rock was located. Professor Craft then pulled the rock from the clay and said, "No matter how hard you try to hide the rock, it is eventually exposed when the walls come crumbling down." The rock that was hidden so well and looked like it was not going to be a problem was the source of the fall.

"The mess is part of God's plan."

God lets us fail so we can deal with the rocks in our character. We only go so far in our growth before the destructive rocks in our character bring us down. Everything may seem fine and we may have some early success, but eventually, the hidden flaws in our character and thinking will bring us down. No matter how many times we try to cover over our flaws, they will eventually be revealed. The higher our walls of our success grow, the greater the mess they make when they come tumbling down. It's never easy or fun when they come tumbling down, but until they do, we can never grow and reach our fullest potential. God uses those humbling moments of failure to expose our flaws and develop our character. The mess is part of God's plan.

The Disciples—Peter and Judas both had terrible failures. The life and ministry they built while traveling with Jesus was one that very few had the opportunity to achieve. Others envied them for their time with Jesus and for the miracles they performed. The walls of their success grew as they traveled with Jesus, but those walls came crashing down in an instant when they betrayed Jesus. The rocks in their character brought them painfully tumbling down. Judas' destructive rock was greed. He was a thief who stole money regularly from the ministry purse. When given the chance, he betrayed Jesus for thirty pieces of silver. The underlying root of greed was exposed, and the walls came crashing down after Judas betrayed Jesus. Then in shame, he tried to return the money.

Peter's destructive rock was pride. Peter promised Jesus that others would betray him but he never would. He believed he was better than the others and that he could do anything apart from God's help. His destructive pride was exposed when he denied Jesus, and his walls came tumbling down. Peter ran and hid in his remorse.

Both men had destructive rocks that brought the walls of their life tumbling down. Both men felt the remorse and pain of their failures, but each man had a different outcome. Rather than dealing with the rock of greed in his life, Judas took his life. Instead of seeking forgiveness and grace, Judas believed his failure meant he was finished. Peter was also broken and full of remorse, but instead of believing he was finished, he allowed God to use the failure to expose the rock of pride in his life and mold him into a better man.

Peter's remorse turned into repentance and he became a better man. The cocky and arrogant Peter was humbled but ready to rise to new levels of influence and leadership. Jesus told Peter earlier in their friendship that in the future, Peter would become a great leader *(Matt 16:18)*. That's exactly what happened. Peter went on to become the catalyst of the early church. His influence as an Apostle would not have happened if Jesus had not exposed the destructive rock of pride in his life.

It's hard to see the rock in your own lump of clay. We try our best to deny our character flaws. We even deny we have any issues until it's obvious to us and everyone around us after our life is torn apart by our failures.

Failure makes the rock in your clay obvious. Once the rock is exposed, you have a choice. You can remove it and start over with the greater potential than you had before or you can try again without the rock removed. You already know the outcome of leaving the rock in the clay. It will come tumbling down again. You may actually get a little further in the process and look like you are going to make it, but the rock will eventually come out and everything will collapse.

If you're in the midst of a painful failure, have you taken the time to ask God what He wants to remove from your life? If not, start doing that now. Take the time to ask Him, "God, what's the rock you want to remove from my life?" When He reveals it, thank Him for his work in your life, offer your rock to Him and ask Him to take it away. For an even more meaningful moment, find a real rock. If possible, write on it a word that symbolizes the thing God wants to remove from your life. Then, after praying, toss it as far as you can into a lake or river. Let the act symbolize your belief that God is using your failure to remove the rock from your life and the hope that He is going to create good from the bad.

God still makes good from bad. When you are dealing with your own failure and the pieces of your life are lying in a pile on the potter's wheel, it's hard to recognize that God is going to bring good from this bad. At the moment, all you can see is the heap of mess. All you feel is the pain of failure. However, God will create good from the bad if you will look inward and ask God what it is that He wants to remove from your lump of clay.

Your failure doesn't mean you're finished. It's part of the process God uses to mold you into the shape He has planned for you. The beauty of the clay is that even after it's collapsed and formless on the table, it can be used again. The process of reusing old clay is called "reclaiming." The word "reclaim" means "to recover (substances) in a pure or usable form for refuse."[1] When the crafter reclaims the lump of clay, he must give careful attention and remove all the impurities from the clay and then add the needed water to soften the clay. After the clay has been "reclaimed," it can once again be crafted into any form the creator desires, but this time, it has the potential to become something greater because the rock has been removed.

God wants to "reclaim" you. He desires to form you into someone even greater than you were before. Take the time to remove any "rocks" from your life and allow God to apply his refreshing water of forgiveness to your broken spirit. In time, you will see God really does create good from bad.

QUESTIONS

1. How has God used failure in your past to shape you?

2. What rocks in your character might God want to expose through your current failures? If you aren't sure, take the time to ask Him. Ask, "God, what's the rock you want to remove from my life?"

POST IT NOTES

Once, I attended a retreat for a small group of Pastors that was led by my friend, David Zimmerman. David leads a ministry to help coach Pastors to understand their calling and learn how to introduce needed growth into churches. At the retreat, David led us to do a project that made a significant impact on my life and it involved Post-it Notes. He instructed us to take the time to write down each of the major events we could remember in our life on a separate yellow Post-It. They could be good events or painful events, but we had to write each of them down. After we finished writing them, we stuck each note to a poster board in chronological order. The board was full of yellow post-its. It was a visual reminder of all the major events in my life… good and bad.

After we placed the events in order, David instructed us to go back through the events and pick the three most painful events and transfer them on to blue post-its. There were quite a lot to choose from, but I eventually picked my three and placed them back in order on the board. Those three events were neatly evenly spaced out over the years, and they looked like special markers in my life. I had no idea how much they truly were valuable markers in my life, but I was about to find out.

David directed us to take the time to think about the three events and then ask ourselves what "good" came from the event. At first, I thought "I can't think of anything good that came from this," but he asked us to consider what it taught us about ourselves, about God and how it developed us. After we took some time to reflect, we wrote our answers on the Post-Its and placed it back on the poster board. After stepping back and looking at the board, it became very evident that those three events positively shaped me more than any of the positive events. It became very obvious to me that God can always bring good from bad and that I need to change the way I look at failures or hardships in my life.

God will bring good from your failure if you take the time to listen and grow. Perhaps you've never taken the time to see how God has used your past failures for good. Just as I took the time to see how God was working in my past, I encourage you to do the same. Make a list your failures. Trust me. It won't be a pretty list, but it will be a helpful list. After you've made the list, pick out three of your biggest failures. Then ask yourself the three questions at the end of this section.

After you've answered the questions, take a few moments to observe how God has used your past failures for your good. You will see He IS working all things for your good. You may not see it yet, but if you're His, you can be sure God will bring good from the bad.

QUESTIONS

1. What did I learn about myself?
2. What did I learn about God?
3. How did this event make me a better person?

CHAPTER 5

BOUNCE BACK

"It's not how far you fall,

but how high you bounce that counts."

- Zig Ziglar[1]

PETER OR JUDAS

It's never easy to bounce back from a failure. I know because for three years, I've been trying to bounce back from failing to meet personal deadlines I've set for writing this book. I've set more deadlines than I can remember. I've missed each one. That's not good when you are writing a book about failure. I even stopped telling people I was writing a book so they would quit asking me about it. With each missed deadline, I've felt more and more like a failure. The sad thing is that I can't quit. You can't write a book about overcoming failure and not finish the book.

I really want to finish the book. I want to finish it so I can help others and because I believe God wants me to write it. The problem is I've failed so many times I'm tempted to quit trying. I actually did quit for six months, but something won't let me quit.

So, here I am writing again. What changed? Nothing really changed in my surroundings. I'm still busy pastoring a church, raising four kids and trying to stay healthy. I'm busier than I've ever been. The thing that changed was my mindset. I made a choice to finish the book. I decided to bounce back from my failure and finish what I started.

A great thing about failure is that we have the option to choose how we will respond to it. We aren't locked into a response. Each of us can choose how to react to our own failures. Some people allow their failure to knock the wind out of them. Others resolve to bounce-back.

Peter and Judas both failed Jesus, and each had an option as to how they would respond to their failure. Judas chose death and Peter chose to bounce-back. You can also choose to bounce back from your failure.

Some of you may have a problem with the word "choose." For those whose theology is firmly rooted in words like "sovereignty," "election" and "predestination," you have a hard time with that word. I also believe those things. I believe in them strongly. The Bible clearly teaches those things, but it also teaches that our choices have a real impact.

"You have a choice in how you will respond to your failure."

Jesus consistently challenged people to make choices. Why? Because your choices have real meaning. You may be thinking, "There's no reason to bounce back. My failure is just part of God's plan for me and I'm just going to have to live in my failure." If that's what you are thinking, you've made an agreement with the enemy. You believe a lie. The truth is you have a choice in how you will respond to your failure. You can choose life or you can choose death. You can choose to do nothing or you can choose to bounce back.

You may be saying, "Okay. Then how do I bounce back?" I'm glad you asked. The rest of this chapter is about bouncing back. I'll be sharing several things you can do to bounce back from your failure. So, if you are ready to choose to bounce back, keep reading. If not, put down the book, but keep it close. You'll need it again soon.

QUESTIONS

1. What are your biggest obstacles to bouncing back from your failure?

2. The big question is, "Do you really want to bounce back and are you willing to do whatever it takes?

EXPECT THE BEST

I could hear the muffled music coming from the old rock chapel down the hill. It sounded like a garage band practicing songs, but I wasn't sure. I would find out soon that what I heard was more than music. It was an anthem. An anthem of faith.

I had been invited to visit and tour a recovery home for men in addiction. A friend who was a member of our church and board member of the recovery home asked for several months for me to join him on a visit to Victory Home in Tallulah Falls, Georgia. I cleared my schedule and dedicated a day to go and see this place he was so passionate about. I was about to find out why he was so impassioned about this place.

As we arrived on the campus of Victory Home, I wasn't sure what to expect. I anticipated seeing broken and depressed men. I expected to see their faces joyless and passionless, but that wasn't what I experienced. Instead, I saw men smiling and laughing. They were full of life and passion. They didn't seem like men who were at the end of their rope who came to this place looking for freedom from addiction to alcohol, drugs and pornography.

These men had failed. They lost their jobs, their families, and their dreams to terrible addictions. This was their last hope. I expected to see men who had given up. Instead, they reminded me of excited teens at a youth camp. They seemed full of hope. Full of life. Full of faith.

I was invited to meet the Directors and join the men for

lunch. The men greeted me with smiles and handshakes. The men in the program prepared a warm lunch for us, and we sat around the round tables telling stories and chatting. Each had his own story of failure. There were single men and married men. There were young men who became addicts in high school. There were older men with families who became addicted to prescription drugs or alcohol later in life. They had families and careers that were now a mess. They had people who no longer wanted to be a part of their lives. Most had very little to look forward to when leaving Victory Home.

After touring the facility and meeting the men, I was invited to the chapel for the daily chapel service. As we approached the old rock-faced building that sat down the hill, I heard the music again. This time it was obvious, that it was the worship band getting ready to lead us in worship. When I sat down near the back of the fifty-year-old stone building with low-hanging wooden beams, I watched as all the men came into the room and sat near the front.

On the stage were several of the men I saw eating moments earlier in the cafeteria. They had guitars strung around their necks; drumsticks in their hands and microphones on stands ready to sing. The men about to lead us in worship were all ages and from all walks of life. One young man had half his head shaved and tattoos covered his body. A couple of the men looked like they might have been carpenters and the pianist looked clean-cut like he might have had a nice job in an office. I'd never seen such a diverse group of men on stage about to lead worship.

After everyone entered and it was time to start, the worship the leader, covered in tattoos and a face that looked worn from abuse, asked everyone to stand and join him in singing. Then it hit me, "I'm about to be led in worship by a group of addicts." All the men on the stage were men in the addiction recovery program. They were all addicts. I've worked in churches twenty years and worked with lots of worship leaders, and there's always the emphasis on being a pure vessel through which the Holy Spirit can flow in worship. But now, I was about to be led in worship by drug dealers, thieves and criminals. The band-of-misfits was about to lead us into the presence of God through worship. I didn't know what to expect. I didn't know I was about to be led in the most genuine worship I had ever experienced.

The men onstage played and sang with true humility and genuine joy. The men in the crowd sang with lifted hands and proud voices. As I watched the raw and unhindered worship of the men, I began to cry. I'm not a crier. I rarely cry. I cry in inspiring movies and kid's movies about Dads. Now, I was crying in a group of men that held nothing back in their love for God. It was beautiful. It was moving.

When I thought it couldn't get any better, they sang a song that I'll never forget. The humble man holding the microphone with his heavily tattooed arms talked a moment about God's grace and then introduced the next song, "Redeemed" by Big Daddy Weave.[1] The song describes the freedom people experience when they are redeemed by Jesus from their failures. The words of the song struck me because they weren't just the words of a random song. The words connected with the men's souls and flowed off their lips like they wrote it. Imagine this group of misfit worship leaders singing with genuine gratefulness to God. It was an experience you will never forget.

The worship leader sang the song with such authenticity and passion. The men in the room joined in and they sang so loud you could hardly hear your own voice.

The men sang the song with conviction and joy. The song wasn't just another worship song with the words projected onto the wall. It was an anthem of freedom. The words connected to their story. It was their story. They were the redeemed ones. They knew it. They believed it. They were letting the whole world know it.

The men in that room knew they were redeemed; they had been set free. They had thrown off the heavy chains! They were no longer named by shame and regret because they knew God was not done with them yet! It was an unforgettable moment. It was a little of what Heaven is going to look like.

So, how did those men who ended up in a place for those who've failed big time end up so full of joy and hope? How did they overcome their failure, find joy again and worship God with such passion? They were able to do it because they had FAITH. The Bible describes faith this way, "Now faith is confidence in what we hope for and assurance about what we do not see."[2] When you've hit the bottom and things are so dark you can't see your way forward, you need to have faith. You need to have confidence and assurance that there is a brighter future ahead even though you can't see it. You need to believe God's grace is sufficient enough to cover all your failures and work all things for your good. You have to believe He's not finished with you. The drive to keep going and to try again comes from confident faith.

There's another word I like to use for faith. It's the word OPTIMISM. Optimism means, "hopefulness and confidence about the future or the successful outcome of something."[3] Being hopeful and confident about our failures isn't something that comes naturally to most of us. Our minds tend to go to the worst possible outcome instead of the best possible outcome. When we fail, we believe we are finished, unwanted or unable to change. We imagine losing the people we love, being rejected or living in a van down by the river. Failure brings out the worst in our imagination. We have a hard time imagining an outcome that will work out for good, but that is the difference faith makes. That is the difference optimism makes. Optimism is the greatest form of faith. Optimism means you believe God will turn your worst situation into the greatest possible outcome.

"Optimism is the greatest form of faith."

Failure is overcome with optimism. Without optimism, you'll believe you're finished and you will go nowhere. When you're optimistic, you aren't just hoping things will turn out well. You KNOW things will turn out well. With optimism, you find the courage and strength to move forward even if you've experienced unimaginable failure. Optimism is the fuel that propels you forward after you've failed the first time or the hundredth time.

The men in that worship-filled room were full of optimism. They were confident that God was not finished with them. They couldn't see the future any more than you and I can, but they had full assurance that God is going to work all things for their good.

My faith seemed small compared to theirs. When things are going well, I have a lot of optimism. It's easy to be optimistic when I'm succeeding, but when things aren't going fine, my confidence dries up like an empty well. I want their optimism. We all need their optimism.

There's no failure too big that God can't handle. He's not sitting around scratching His head trying to figure out how to fix your problem. He's still in control and He's still working. He has a plan and He's not finished.

Have you lost all hope? Have you given yourself over to doom and gloom? If so, it's time to leave despair behind and be optimistic. Jump in with both feet and have the faith to believe in what you can't see. Have the faith to be hopeful about yourself and believe your future is going to be greater than your past.

QUESTIONS

1. What outcome do you expect to come from your failure? Would you describe it as an optimistic or pessimistic point of view?

2. Can you think of five reasons you should have an optimistic view of your future?

3. How can you start today to have a more optimistic view of your future?

SELF-COMPASSION

I love food and I hate food. I'm a "Foodie." That means I love to eat great tasting food. Actually, I can't think of any food I don't like. I love traveling to try new foods, new restaurants, and new recipes. There's no problem with loving food, but I also like to eat lots of food. There's a problem with that.

Just as much as I love food, I also hate food. I hate the power I let it have over my life. Like many people, I fight a constant battle to eat healthy and to eat only what I need. I've struggled for years to maintain a healthy weight. My weight and my fitness level have changed more than a politician's opinion.

Taking care of my body is important to me. As a Christian, I believe I'm called to honor God with my body and take care of it. I also want to actively live in this body for a long time. After all, if I don't take care of it, where else am I going to live? I desire to stay active, play and use my mind and body a long time for God. The problem is, I have this insatiable appetite for food.

I eat because I like the way food tastes, but I also eat because I like the way food makes me feel, at least temporarily. I'm an emotional eater. I eat when I'm sad, and I eat when I'm glad. I eat when I'm bored and I eat when I'm excited. As a matter of fact, there's not an emotion that I haven't tied to eating. I can always find a reason to eat. There's a word for this type of behavior. The word is GLUTTONY. I'm a glutton and I don't like it.

There's a reason the Bible calls gluttony a sin. Gluttony robs us of our ability to do the things we want to do and the things God calls us to do. It also keeps us from finding authentic healing in our soul. We use food to medicate real emotional and spiritual problems that need to be addressed if we want to truly be healthy and whole. I know these things, but I still battle eating too much and too often.

When it comes to gluttony, I'm a failure. Like I've said before, I should be a professional Failure. I've been a failure in this area just about my whole life. I feel like I fail in this part of my life on a daily basis, and each time I fail, I feel the same toxic emotions of self-pity and self-condemnation.

Self-pity and self-condemnation are common emotions many of us feel when we fail. It's easy to tell ourselves how awful we are when we fail, and when you are a glutton, you are

"Self-condemnation and self-pity never helped anyone."

reminded of your failure each time you look in the mirror. When we are faced with our own failure, we are inclined to condemn and ridicule ourselves.

When we fail, we beat ourselves up terribly. We call ourselves names, get depressed and treat ourselves harshly. I mean why not? You're the only one to blame. No one made you eat three pieces of cake. You did it yourself. But, should you beat yourself up? Should you feel self-condemnation and self-pity when you fail? The answer is no.

Self-condemnation and self-pity never helped anyone. Self-condemnation and self-pity continue a cycle that never lets us escape our failure. It often leads right back to the same destructive failure. If our failure is a moral failure, James 4:7-10 tells us to feel the weight of our sin, but our failure only turns to growth if we move beyond remorse and let God lift us up.

If you desire to move beyond remorse, self-pity and self-condemnation, there's something better you must give yourself. To move forward, you need SELF- COMPASSION. In his article in the Harvard Business Review, Christopher Germer says this about self-compassion, "There is a substantial and growing body of research that shows that self-compassion is closely associated with emotional resilience, including the ability to soothe ourselves, recognize our mistakes, learn from them, and motivate ourselves to succeed. Self-compassion is consistently correlated with a wide range of measures of emotional well-being such as optimism, life satisfaction, autonomy, and wisdom, as well as with reduced levels of anxiety, depression, stress, and shame."[1] Self-Compassion redirects our mind and attitude. It gets our thoughts and emotions headed in a healthy direction.

Kristin Neff describes Self-compassion as showing yourself the same compassion you would show a close friend.[2] It's amazing how much compassion we have for a close friend when they fail. When friends come to us hurting, most people will accept them, encourage them and help them see beyond their failure. We are pretty good at showing compassion to others but we are terrible at showing it to our self.

Jesus commands us to "love your neighbor as yourself,"[3] but when we fail, we frequently treat our neighbor better than we treat ourselves. To fully carry out Jesus' command, you have to show yourself as much compassion as you show others. You have to love yourself the way you love others.

I once had a staff member who worked for me at my church that remorsefully confessed to me that he failed me big time. He said he envied my position and thought he could do a better job leading. He then went on to say he actually prayed that I would fail in ministry. After I wanted to punch him, I saw through his tears and sorrow and I could sense his repentance. Instead of scorning him or condemning him, I quickly forgave him and encouraged him. It's amazing how easily and quickly we show others compassion when they fail but it's hard for us to show ourselves the same grace and forgiveness.

Why can't we have the same compassion for our self just like we have for others? I believe when we experience moral failure, we have a hard time having self-compassion because we haven't fully grasped what Jesus did for us on the cross.

We frequently feel we have to pay for our failure by being self-critical and self-condemning. It's as if we think we can actually make things right by feeling worse about our self. I've got news for you. You've never made anything better by feeling bad about yourself, and you've never improved on the work of God by being self-condemning.

The truth is that the work Jesus did on the cross is enough to cover all your failures. Your past, present and future failures are covered by the sacrificial blood of Jesus. The Bible declares, "But when the Priest (Jesus) had offered for all time one sacrifice for sins, he sat down at the right hand of God."[4] Jesus made one sacrifice for you that covered all your sin, and no amount of self-pity or self-condemnation is needed to cover your sin. The sacrifice is so complete that Jesus sat down as if to say my work is finished.

Jesus made you perfect through His work on the cross. You may not be perfect in your actions, but in the eyes of God, you have been made perfect. Read this verse. Read it slowly and let what it says soak in. "For by one sacrifice he has made perfect forever those who are being made holy."[5]

Did you see that? Did you see what that verse says about you? It says you are "perfect forever." If God sees you as perfect, there's no need to condemn and ridicule yourself. Have self-compassion! The verse also says you are "being made holy. " You are already perfect but you are also being made holy. God sees you as perfect

"We are pretty good at showing compassion to others but we are terrible at showing it to our self."

but you're also in process. You are in process of becoming what God says you already are. Your failure is part of the process God is using to make you holy. Quit beating yourself up! See yourself as God sees you and have some compassion.

So the question is: "How do you have self-compassion?" It's simple. Treat yourself like you would a close friend. If a close friend sorrowfully came to you after having failed you, what would you say and do? I bet you'd forgive them and encourage them. That's the same thing you should do for yourself. When you fail, you need encouragement, and you may need forgiveness. The best person to give you those two things is you.

No matter how many times you fail, you still need to forgive yourself. Even if you fail seven times in a day and repent each time, you still need to have self-compassion and forgive yourself. How do I know this? I know it because Jesus taught His disciples to have unlimited forgiveness for a person that repents. In Luke 17:3-4, Jesus instructed His disciples to forgive someone who sinned against them even if they repeated the offense seven times in one day.

The number seven is significant because throughout the Bible, it represents completion. In other words, forgive the person until the forgiveness is complete no matter how many times they offend you. If we are told to forgive our neighbor that many times, aren't we also supposed to forgive our self just as many times? After all, you're supposed to love your neighbor as much as you love yourself.

In order to bounce back, you need to have the self-compassion that allows you to forgive yourself. You need to let yourself off the hook and let it go. You failed and you're going to live.

There's something else you can do to have self-compassion. To have self-compassion, you need to encourage yourself just as you would a good friend. There's power in words you speak to others. Words of encouragement from a friend have helped many people get out of a pit. The words you speak to yourself are just as powerful.

Instead of condemning and ridiculing yourself, speak words to yourself that bring healing. Proverbs 12:18 describes the power of your words. It says, "The words of the reckless pierce like swords, but the tongue of the wise brings healing."[6] Your words have the power to destroy or heal. The words you speak to yourself are either building you up or tearing you down.

Can I be honest with you? I still struggle with this. When I fail at something, which is regularly, I catch myself saying "I hate myself. I'm such a loser." I don't hate myself and I don't really think I'm a loser, but when I fail, I constantly have to check my words. I would never say those things to a friend that failed. I should never say them to myself.

How are you doing with the words you speak to yourself? Are they words that bring healing, encouragement and hope? Or do your words make you sick, discourage you and cause you to lose hope? You have the power over your words. It's time to have self-compassion.

If you are struggling with having self-compassion, I have something I want you to do. Pretend you are writing a letter to a friend in your situation. What would say to that person? How would you counsel him or her? How would you encourage him or her? Now, write a letter to yourself using the same words. Find out what it's like to have self-compassion and start to heal.

QUESTIONS

1. How would you define "Self-Compassion?"
2. What's the difference between how you treat a friend who failed and how you treat yourself when you fail?
3. How would you treat yourself differently if you treated yourself like a friend that failed?

REVIVER

Failure sucks the life and energy right out of you. It makes you want to throw the towel in the ring and quit trying. It's like my two sons when they play video games. Often, when they are playing a game against one another, one of them will start outscoring the other by a large amount. When that happens, an argument starts nearly every time. The one losing gets so frustrated he jumps up and turns the game off leaving the other one mad and angry. A heated argument between the two of them always follows. They both hate it when the game is turned off on them, but they continue to do so to each other. Why? Because failing makes you want to quit. It robs you of your passion, strength and energy. It is hard to keep moving forward.

When you fail and want to quit, your heart needs to be revived. Revive means "to restore to life; regain strength; give new energy."[1] The good news is, your heart can be revived when you've failed. Your failure doesn't mean you're finished. You can be restored to life. You can regain your strength and be given new energy. How do I know? I know because the God of the Bible is a REVIVER. He is in the business of reviving broken hearts and spirits. Look at what the Bible says in Isaiah 57:15, "For this is what the high and exalted One says—he who lives forever, whose name is holy: "I live in a high and holy place, but also with the one who is contrite and lowly in spirit, to revive the spirit of the lowly and to revive the heart of the contrite."[2]

Our God is the Reviver of tired, broken and cold hearts. No

matter how low, broken and stuck you feel, God is near you and can revive your heart. You may be thinking, "But I'm far too gone. I messed up big time! God doesn't want to revive me." When you've morally failed, it's easy to believe you're finished, but God has a lot to say to the person who thinks he or she is too far gone.

Jesus told a parable about a young man who thought he was too far gone and who was in desperate need of reviving after he failed. In Luke 15, Jesus tells the story of a young man that despised his upbringing and disrespected his father. When the son decided he wanted to be on his own, he asked for his inheritance before his father had even passed away. In essence, he was saying to his Father, "you are dead to me and I just want your money." His father graciously gave him his inheritance and the son left. The son rebelliously left the blessing and covering of his father's household and lived a wild life wasting all of the inheritance the Father gave him.

When he finally had nowhere to go and his friends left him, he ended up working with filthy pigs. He hit the lowest point he could possibly hit. He was at rock bottom. It was then he became very aware of his own major failure, and the rocks in his character were revealed. His life was a mess but in his failure, he remembered the love of his father. He then decided he would return home and offer to be a servant in his father's home.

He felt lifeless, embarrassed and like he was finished, but he returned home anyway. Luke described what happens next. "So he returned home to his father. And while he was still a long way off, his father saw him coming. Filled with love and compassion, he ran to his son, embraced him, and kissed him."[3]

Did you notice the love in the Father's response? It's totally different than what we expect from a Father that has been disrespected and rejected. Instead of anger and bitterness, he was "filled with love and compassion." He "ran to his son, embraced him, and kissed him." Jesus beautifully describes the love of the Father in this story.

Can you imagine the shocked response of the son? He probably thought his Father was running toward him in anger and that he wanted to kill him. When his Father embraced him and kissed him, he undoubtedly felt so small but so loved.

> "Nothing can separate you from the love of God..."

The humbled son then shows us exactly what it looks like to come back to the Father when we've failed. Look at what he says, "His son said to him, 'Father, I have sinned against both heaven and you, and I am no longer worthy of being called your son.'"[4] There's a word for what the son did. It's called REPENTANCE. Repentance means to turn from sin and dedicate oneself to the amendment of one's life.[5] The son returned to the father broken and ready to change. Look at how the father responded to him, "But his father said to the servants, 'Quick! Bring the finest robe in the house and put it on him. Get a ring for his finger and sandals for his feet. And kill the calf we have been fattening. We must celebrate with a feast, for this son of mine was dead and has now returned to life. He was lost, but now he is found.' So the party began."[6]

This is such a stunning picture of grace and forgiveness. The father didn't give him what he deserved. He gave him the love he didn't deserve and the gifts he didn't expect. The loving father "revived" him. He restored him to life, gave him a new start and renewed his strength. That's what the Heavenly Father will also do for you.

Jesus shows us in this story that you're never too far gone for a fresh start, and His love for His children knows no end. The Apostle Paul said this about God's far-reaching love, "Who shall separate us from the love of Christ? Shall trouble or hardship or persecution or famine or nakedness or danger or sword? ...³⁸For I am convinced that neither death nor life, neither angels nor demons, neither the present nor the future, nor any powers, ³⁹neither height nor depth, nor anything else in all creation, will be able to separate us from the love of God that is in Christ Jesus our Lord."[7]

Nothing can separate you from the love of God in Christ Jesus. Your sin is great, but God's love is greater. His love revives lifeless hearts, renews strength and gives you a new energy, but there's something you have to do. To get a fresh start, you have to humbly return to the Father. If you are ready to be revived, decide that you are willing to change and do things differently. Resolve that you are ready to deal with the rocks in your clay and return to the Father. When you do that, times of refreshing will come from the Lord. Acts 3:19 says, "Repent, then, and turn to God, so that your sins may be wiped out, that times of refreshing may come from the Lord,"[8]

Are you ready for refreshing times? Are you ready to be revived, restored and renewed? If so, humbly return to the Lord and then confess your failures and your flaws. Restoration doesn't happen without repentance. When you return to the Father with humble repentance, He showers you with His love and favor. Before you move on, confess your sins to the Father and agree to make the needed changes to become a different person.

Perhaps your failure had nothing to do with your sin. Maybe it was someone else's sin that led to the failure of your marriage or your ministry. Even so, return to the father and be revived. If the loving Father can shower His rebellious son with grace and gifts and then restore him to a place of prominence, He will surely revive you. Your failure does not equal finished. Humbly turn to the Father and let Him embrace you with His love.

QUESTIONS

1. What word would you use to describe the condition of your heart right now? Does it need reviving?
2. Are there things you need to confess to God and repent of so times of refreshing may come to you? If so, take the time to do it now.

LABELS

Labels are important. They help us define things, and it's frustrating when the label doesn't accurately describe the product. When I was sixteen, I took my first trip to Atlanta in my own car with my friends to hang out, have some fun and feel grown-up. While roaming the streets of Atlanta one evening, a man approached us and asked if we wanted to purchase a great watch for a really cheap price. The word "cheap" got my attention. We followed the man to his stand hid away in the alley. He opened the cabinet and revealed many brand-named wristwatches. I spotted the one I wanted. It looked great and it had the great name brand label to go with it. The watch looked like an original. The label alone said it was an authentic expensive watch.

After we settled on a price, I purchased my brand new watch for $20. I walked away as the proud new owner of a new fancy wristwatch. I wore it on my wrist with pride. I was a proud young teenager who could drive himself to the big city and score a great deal on a fancy watch.

My pride didn't last very long. Within a week, my fancy new wristwatch stopped working. The hands stopped working and a new battery didn't fix the problem. I had been duped, and my teenage pride turned to teenage regret. Through that debacle, I learned a valuable lesson: Labels don't always accurately describe what's on the inside. Labels are important, but it's crucial that the label accurately describes what's on the inside.

Like the products we buy, we also have labels. We have obvious labels like Dad, Mom, friend, son, daughter, employee, athlete, artist, Christian and so forth. We also have labels that we use to define ourselves that aren't so obvious to others. These labels are printed in our hearts and minds. These are the labels we use to define ourselves. We don't often share our labels with others, but in our inner self, we hear our names. Like false labels on a wristwatch, there are times when our labels don't always accurately describe what's on the inside. These false labels frequently come to us at times of hurt, disappointment, and failure.

I know about fighting false labels. I fight against my own false labels constantly. I love cycling. It's one of the best ways I've found to stay in shape, have fun and spend some time alone talking to God. Recently, while road cycling at the beach, I had to fight the urge to label myself a failure.

Usually, my rides are a time to clear my mind, but not this time. I had just ridden about twenty miles into a strong headwind and turned around to head back. My teen daughter's boyfriend was riding inches behind me, and we were both exhausted. We began our twenty-mile return trip and we were pedaling as hard as we could, but traffic began to slow behind us. There was one red truck that wouldn't pass even though they had plenty of room to pass. We pedaled hard to get out of their way and we were unable to get on the sidewalk because of our high speed and the crowded sidewalks.

Once we were able to find a wider section on the road, I pulled over as far as I could and the truck pulled up beside me.

I looked to my left and the truck's window was down. In that window there was a woman about my age hanging halfway out and screaming profanities at me! Immediately, I did what every Jesus-loving Pastor does. I prayed for her. No. Not really…I shot her a bird! Right there before I even knew what I did. I let my anger get the best of me and I did something I've not done in decades. I flipped her off! Now, that might be something you do all the time, but not me. I'm pretty careful not to let my road rage get the best of me. I'm a Pastor for goodness sake. Now, I'm not just a Pastor. I'm now the Bird Shooting Pastor! Seconds later, I realized my daughter's boyfriend was inches behind me and probably saw the whole thing. I decided not to look back and see his shocked face. Instead, I took off after the truck not really knowing what I would do if I caught them. I left the boyfriend in the dust and I never caught the truck, but my actions caught up with me soon enough when guilt and shame came rushing over me.

I, the Pastor, just lost my cool, shot someone a bird and my daughter's boyfriend watched the entire thing. After my lungs could no longer take the pace and my legs began to burn, I slowed down, but the guilt of my deed caught up with me. Instantly, I began to label myself. Labels like Loser, Hypocrite, and Failure began to flood my mind. For the next few miles, I sulked in my failure. What I did wasn't right. It was wrong. I knew it. I felt it. I hated myself for it. I may have acted that way, but that's not who I am because I know who I am in Christ.

Labels are sticky. I've always hated it when retailers stick a label on something I want to purchase. I can't tell you how much time I've wasted trying to get the annoyingly sticky residue off something left there from a sticker. Just like labels on a package, the labels we allow to be stuck on us are hard to remove. When we label ourselves or are tempted to label ourselves, we have to be careful because those labels are hard to get off once we've allowed them to stick.

You may be thinking: *well, what's wrong with labels*? The problem with labels is that we act in accordance with who we believe we are. If the label doesn't match who you truly are, you'll be constantly frustrated. Your heart is the place where the labels stick. Be careful. The labels you allow to be stuck on your heart will impact

"You act in accordance with who you believe you are."

everything you do. We looked at this verse before, but look again at what it says, "Above all else, guard your heart, for everything you do flows from it."[1]

Everything you do flows from your heart. If in your heart you believe you are a failure, then everything you do will be impacted by it. Your future success, relationships and efforts will all be influenced by the failure label you wear on your heart.

You act in accordance with who you believe you are. After you've failed, you have to be careful to guard your heart from the false labels you and others want to place on it! Make sure the labels you use accurately describe who you really are.

It's essential that the labels you wear match what's on the inside or you'll never reach the full potential of whom you really are. You'll never know the hope, the riches and the power God gives you. To overcome failure, you have to identify your false labels and identify yourself by the labels God gives you.

That's what the Apostle Paul wanted the churches he started to understand. In Ephesians 1, the Apostle Paul is writing to the church. In his letter, he reveals a prayer that he is praying for them. In his prayer, he describes his desire for them to see things about God and themselves the way they are meant to be seen. Look here at what he says, "I have not stopped giving thanks for you, remembering you in my prayers. I keep asking that the God of our Lord Jesus Christ, the glorious Father, may give you the Spirit of wisdom and revelation, so that you may know him better. I pray that the eyes of your heart may be enlightened in order that you may know the hope to which he has called you, the riches of his glorious inheritance in his holy people, and his incomparably great power for us who believe." Ephesian 1:16-19 (NIV)[2]

Paul desires for the church in Ephesus to see with spiritual eyes beyond what they see and think with their natural mind. He asks for the Spirit of God to give unto them more wisdom and revelation. He also requests that the "eyes of your heart may be enlightened" so that they may see things they had not seen before. Each of us needs to have the "eyes of our heart" opened so that we can see the things God wants us to see about Him and ourselves.

In essence, Paul is saying we need help seeing. We especially need help seeing ourselves as God sees us. You may be wondering why you need help seeing yourself as God sees you. You need help seeing yourself as God sees you because you are not who you think you are. You are who God says you are. Don't miss that. Read it again. You are not who you think you are. You are who God says you are.

Your spiritual eyes can be blinded by the labels you've allowed to be printed on your heart. Your past experiences and the voices of others easily influence who you think you are. If you've experienced failure after failure, it's easy to label yourself a failure. Then that label becomes a self-fulfilling prophecy in your life.

"You are not who you think you are. You are who God says you are."

Paul's prayer is that you would begin to see yourself as God sees you. He wants you to identify yourself by the label God gives you and no other. He wants you to understand who you really are.

Too many of us have labels that don't match who we really are. We think we are one thing and God says we are something else. Paul says the eyes of our heart need to be opened so we can really see God and ourselves.

In order to move on and allow God to bring the best from your failure, it's important that you rewrite the labels on your heart. Like pulling off old sticky labels that have been stuck for years, you have to do the work of peeling back the false labels and replacing them with the labels God gives you.

You need to see yourself as God sees you. How can you do that? Paul gives us a clue right here in this scripture. The same prayer Paul prayed for the church is the same prayer you can pray for yourself. If you really want to see yourself as God sees you, pray the same thing Paul prayed for you.

Paul prayed that you would receive more of the Spirit of

Wisdom and Revelation. This is God's Spirit, which He freely gives to all at salvation. However, Paul asks that you would receive more wisdom and revelation from Him. In order to see yourself as God sees you, ask God to give you more of the wisdom that comes from His Holy Spirit. The Bible clearly states, "If any of you lacks wisdom, you should ask God, who gives generously to all without finding fault, and it will be given to you." James 1:5 (NIV)

You need wisdom from God to understand things you would not know unless God showed you. There is man's wisdom and there is God's wisdom. God's wisdom is so much higher and greater than ours. It sees deep within us and shows us things we would not know unless He reveals it.

Too often, our hearts and our labels are defined by man's "wisdom." My wife Dana was once told by a woman she respected that she would never be successful. Those words crushed her and were a false label someone else tried to put on her. This is man's wisdom, not God's. Thankfully, she has the wisdom of God to see the difference between God's labels and man's labels.

If you want to understand how God sees you and discern between man's wisdom and God's wisdom, ask Him for more of His wisdom and revelation. In doing so, you'll begin to understand who you really are in Christ.

Paul prayed that the eyes of their hearts would be opened and they would see things as God sees them. If you want to see yourself as God sees you, ask God to open the eyes of your heart. As God begins to show you your false labels, start the work of replacing those labels with who God says you are. At the end of this book, there is a list of scripture that define who you are in Christ. Take the time to read through them and begin to confront your false labels with the true labels God gives you. It's time to walk in your true identity. You are not who you think you are. You are who God says you are! If you need help seeing yourself the way God sees you, here's a prayer you can pray right now. "God, help me to see you and to see myself as you see me. Expose the false labels I've allowed to determine my identity. Help me to see who I really am."

QUESTIONS

1. Can you name five false labels you've been calling yourself?
2. Take the time to ask God for five new labels He wants to give you.

YOUR PURPOSE

Regaining your vision after you've failed can be difficult. It's hard to see past your failure into the future and believe that anything good will come from your weaknesses. When you're down on the ground and nursing your wounds from a fall, it's not easy to think about getting back up again and running your race. However, running again is exactly what you need to do. Falling should not keep you from running again. As stated earlier in the book, the writer of Proverbs said this... "though the righteous fall seven times, they rise again..." Proverbs 24:16 (NIV)

Failure shouldn't keep you from running again. The best runners fall but get back up again, again and again. This scripture doesn't say losers or failures fall seven times and get back up again. It says the "righteous" or the best people fall many times and they get back up again. In your journey, you will fall, but failure doesn't equal finished.

God still has a plan for you, and your failures become part of your future when you understand that your message is often found in your mess. God uses your mess to give you direction for your life. Earlier in the book, I shared how God uses failure for good in your life. He often uses it to guide you into your calling.

When we fail God, ourselves or others, we try to hide our weaknesses. We're embarrassed and ashamed by our failures, but the world needs Honest Failures. It's in our weaknesses that

God shapes us and He develops us. Then we are to use our lessons to help others.

The Apostle Paul was not afraid to be an Honest Failure. He even boasted in his weakness. Once while writing to the church in Corinth, Paul shared about a weakness he had in his life. We aren't sure what it is, but I believe God wanted to keep it generic so we can all relate to him. Look at what he said about his weakness, "But he said to me, 'My grace is sufficient for you, for my power is made perfect in weakness.' Therefore, I will boast all the more gladly about my weaknesses, so that Christ's power may rest on me." 2 Corinthians 12:9 (NIV)[1]

Paul was not afraid to be honest about his weaknesses. He even said he would boast about his weakness because God's power would be revealed through it. God turns your weaknesses into purpose when you rely on Him. Instead of hiding in shame, you must come to the place where you realize God's power is greater than your failure and He can do what my friend Kathrine Lee says, "God can turn your pain into purpose."

My wife, Dana, has always been one who lived with integrity and who pursued the Lord from an early age. She doesn't have many grand stories about moral failure or losing her temper and chasing people on a bike. She has her own failures that you may be able to relate to. They aren't moral failures, but God has used her flaws and shortcomings to shape her and give her purpose. I'll let her share her story about how God has turned her pain into purpose.

"In 2014, I found myself in a place I never thought I would. I was on top of the world. I had a growing business, growing ministry, and

thriving family. I had been given an opportunity to speak with my business, and I was driving alone to Atlanta on a beautiful spring morning. I was a little tired from recent travel, but I was excited.

As I headed out that morning, I remember praying. I said, 'God, I'm a little tired, but I know I can do this.' I got in my van and headed toward Atlanta. About 10 minutes into my commute, I started to feel a little dizzy and light headed. I assumed I needed something more to eat, so I stopped at a gas station. I purchased what I needed, ate some crackers, and headed on. I was feeling better and decided to make a call.

I was heading into Atlanta where two lanes become six when all of a sudden I started feeling like I was fading, passing out. I quickly hung up the phone and heard the Lord say: 'Drink your water so your body will know you are still in control,' so I did. As cars were passing me on either side, I panicked. I had the fight or flight feeling and I wasn't fighting. I was flight-ing.

I began to pray and ask God to get me off the interstate. I somehow got over and saw a hospital sign at the next exit. I proceeded to exit the interstate and noticed a Home Depot parking lot to the right off the exit. I thought... 'I have to get there.' I kept praying out loud and drinking my water. I made it to the parking lot and parked my car.

I was paralyzed. I did not know what was happening to me. I was terrified. I called a friend that I was supposed to be meeting and she said it sounded like I was having a panic attack. This was ridiculous. I wasn't stressed. I was fine. Things were good. This didn't make sense.

As I sat there paralyzed, I called Randall. I burst into tears and told him I didn't know what was going on but the thought of driving back home made me feel like I was going to pass out again. When I say I was paralyzed, I mean I could not move. In Randall's calming way, he said,

"Tell me where you are and I'll come get you and bring you home." A friend brought Randall to me so he could drive my van back home.

I want to pause here and say… I had four active kids, two high school girls, one middle school boy, and one boy in 4ᵗʰ grade. I was burning the candle at both ends taking care of our family, working a growing business, and ministry life as well. Nothing was bad in my life, but I felt like I had to control everything and do everything. My world came crumbling down that day or at least, it felt like it.

Randall got me home and I went straight to bed. The trauma was exhausting and I slept the entire day. I had no energy. After talking to several people, it appeared to be anxiety and a panic attack.

I stayed home the next day, but the day after that, I was supposed to meet this same friend about 20 minutes away. I got in my car…feeling a little anxious but well rested. I headed down the road. Everything was fine. Whew, I was so thankful that it was just a one-time thing. Little did I know that recalling that event while I was driving would cause the same thing to happen again! I immediately called Randall and screamed, 'it is happening again!! Please Pray Randall!' Randall prayed against the enemy. I began to proclaim truth and listen to worship music. I fought the entire way. When I finally got to where I was going, I was exhausted. I was shaking, but I played it off because I felt ridiculous!

I fought it the whole way home but finally made it home. I remember falling on my bed sobbing. I began to ask God what was wrong with me? I wondered if I had something suddenly wrong with my brain? Was it my hormones? There was no explanation. I began to get frustrated and angry. I didn't have time for this in my life. I started going to Doctors to rule out anything specific being wrong. I was perfectly healthy. Everything came back that I was in excellent condition, but I felt terribly wrong.

I stopped driving as much as I could because it was a fight every time I got in the car. Randall was so gracious and never made me feel bad. I could do the short trips to school and back, but that was about it.

I remember one morning, I woke up around 5 AM and immediately thought about me driving my kids to school. I started to panic. Randall woke up because he could tell that something was wrong. I was too embarrassed to tell him that I couldn't even drive my kids to school. I finally burst into tears and he just held me. He got up and took the kids to school.

"God wants to turn your mess in to your message and your pain in to purpose."

When he left that morning, I came into the living room. Jesus and I had to have a conversation. I had never felt so desperate. I laid on the floor and begged and pleaded with God to take this anxiety away from me. I reminded Him of His faithfulness. I reminded Him of His promises and power. After I cried out for a long time, it seemed like hours; I just laid there quiet...Exhausted.

Talk about feeling like a failure. I couldn't even drive my babies to school. Then, in the quiet of my heart and mind, I heard the Lord say, 'Dana, I love you. I have allowed this anxiety for a reason. I am not going to just take this from you like you want me to. You are going to have to walk through this journey...but, I am with you every step of the way and I will never leave you. I want you to walk through this journey so you can help others walk through this journey.' I immediately started crying because I knew how hard this was going to *be and I just wanted to go back to the strong independent woman who was on top of the world. I didn't want this weakness. I didn't want this struggle. I didn't want this pain. Little did I know He wanted to turn my pain into His purpose.*

I felt a leading from the Lord to go to counseling. I felt like there were some underlying fears that could have been related to my anxiety and I was willing to do anything. As I began counseling with New Name Ministries, I began to understand my identity in Jesus. For a long time, I was trying to do so much on my own, and all my hope and identity was in my family, ministry, husband, and business. I had no idea that the foundation of who I was, was so insecure.

I remember an exercise that I had to do in my counseling. I had to ask God where He was during my anxiety attack on my way to Atlanta. He told me He was driving my car for me. He was right there the entire time. He never left me and He never will. This was healing for me. I knew then that part of the purpose of my pain was to understand my identity in Christ and teach others the same. Apart from ANYTHING, I am worthy, whole, healed, secure, important, valuable, called, an heir, His princess, and loved. No matter what.

God is so faithful to use all of our pain and turn it into purpose if we allow Him. He doesn't waste a thing. He bottles up our tears to be poured out. I may have felt like a failure, but I knew God was not finished with me.

Now, God has given me so many opportunities to share my struggle. I don't live from a place of struggle any longer. I live in a place of victory and I can do that because the battle has already been won. We may struggle with things on this earth from time to time but I have learned how to fight against the enemy and his schemes on my life. He has already been defeated. One of the ways I have learned to fight through my anxiety is doing things afraid. Now, I do the hard things anyway.

Do I still struggle? Yes, I do. But I can see the big picture now. In order for God to prepare me for what He has for me, I needed to know my identity in Him. He has used my anxiety to do that. He has also used my story to give others hope. So, whatever your pain is, He will use it for His purpose if you will let Him."

Failure does not equal finished. God wants to turn your mess in to your message and your pain in to purpose. Instead of hiding in shame and remorse, begin to ask God how you can use your failure to help others. Don't be afraid to speak about your weakness. By speaking about your failures, you give others hope and courage to also come back from their failures.

God had a purpose and plan for you. Your failures aren't great enough to mess up God's plans. Offer your failures and strengths to God and watch what He will do through you.

QUESTIONS

1. What are the three ways God could use your failure to help others?

2. Who do you know that has been through what you've passed through and is now thriving?

3. How could you talk with that person about how they turned their pain into purpose?

A HEALING COMMUNITY

Like many Pastors, I'm an introvert. Yes, I regularly speak in front of large crowds, share my life on social media and write material revealing the stories of my life, but when it comes to one-on-one interaction with smaller crowds, I get uncomfortable. I prefer to be more open through Social media, through writing and through public speaking than I do one-on-one with a small group of people. Those forms of communication give me a false form of security. They are all one-way conversations. I'm doing all the talking and there's very little room for pushing deeper in to my soul. Keeping others at a distance feels safe and comfortable because I can control the conversation. Though isolation from others feels safer, I've learned people rarely succeed in isolation.

Though isolation feels safe, it's the furthest thing from safe. Isolating yourself from others keeps people at a distance and keeps you from having to deal with the pain of rejection, disloyalty and embarrassment. It's easier to put on a smile, say everything is okay and hide your insecurities when no one can get close to you.

Isolating yourself after you've failed feels like the safest alternative. The embarrassment of your failure and the humiliation of admitting your personal flaws to someone else is enough to make you want to leave everything and everyone and go live in a van down by the river. Although isolating yourself after you've failed feels like the safest thing, it can be one of the most damaging things you can do. The process of allowing God to use your failure to develop you works best in a community.

Healing is a community project. It's through interaction with others that God's presence becomes more real to you. Other people become God's hands, feet and heart in your life. It's through the community that God begins to heal you and get you back on your feet.

After hitting the rock bottom in my life and nearly walking away from ministry, I decided I would allow more people into my inner life. My old way of interacting with people was not working. It led to depression, anxiety and almost destroyed the ministry to which God had called me. I wanted more from life and did not want to end up in the same place again. Allowing safe people deeper into my life has been one of the most healing things for me and many others. It has allowed God to do His work of removing the rocks and developing His picture in our most vulnerable times.

One of the biggest indicators of someone's success after they've failed is community interaction. Being open and honest with others is one of the last things we want to do when we've been unsuccessful. We are afraid of being embarrassed and humiliated even more, so we push others away. Pushing others away does not lead to growth because healing is a community project. We need one another in the good times and especially in the bad times.

Once, I was leading a group of people through a study based around the material in this book. In our discussion time, I asked them to describe to me what helped them the most to recover from a time when they failed miserably. The group was made up of people who had been divorced multiple times, recovering addicts and other people like you and me who had bombed some areas of their life. As we went around the table and shared, there was a reoccurring theme. Each person shared that being in community with safe and encouraging people helped them recover the most. Community interaction really is one of the best indicators of someone's success after failure.

Think back to the story about Peter and Judas. They both failed miserably. Judas then isolated himself while Peter continued in communion with the other disciples. We know the outcome. Judas' failure and then isolation led to his death. Peter's failure changed his life for the better. After what he did, there's no doubt Peter felt shame and guilt while spending time with the other disciples. Nonetheless, he continued to fellowship with them and allow the community to make him into a better man.

The writer of the Book of Galatians understood the importance of community. In Galatians 6:23, Paul instructed the churches to "Carry each other's burdens, and in this way you will fulfill the law of Christ." Galatians 6:2 (NIV)[1]

Failure is a burden we are to help each other carry. Other people can't help you carry it if you aren't connected to them. When you fail and want to shut yourself away from others, you keep others from being able to fulfill the law of Christ. By allowing others to help you carry your burden of failure, you also allow them to show their love for Christ.

The word "carry" in the Galatians 6:2 means "to take up with hands;" "to carry on one's person."[2] The idea is that as followers of Jesus, we are to help one another lift the heavy load of heavy burdens. We are to take on one another's burdens of failure. We can't do that if we isolate ourselves from one another when we fail.

Faith is strengthened through friendships. When we allow safe friends to help carry the load of our failure, our faith is strengthened and we recover quicker. It's through the care and compassion of people who want the best for us that we see God restore us.

If you desire for God to reclaim you and develop you, then connect to a caring community. Not every friendship or community is a caring community. In Romans 15:5, the Apostle Paul describes two characteristics of a caring community. He

"Failure is a burden we are to help each other carry."

states, "May the God who gives endurance and encouragement give you the same attitude of mind toward each other that Christ Jesus had," Romans 15:5 (NIV)[3]

Paul describes two things that God gives each of us, and then he says we are to show those two things to one another. Caring communities give endurance and encouragement to one another.

Recovering from failure is a humbling and draining experience. It can drain you of all your energy and drive. It's much like running a race. Running a race is difficult when you run it alone. When you've pushed yourself and run your hardest by yourself, it's easy to slow down, walk and even quit. However, if you run a race with someone who believes in you, then you are able to endure to the finish line.

Previously, I shared how I was at one of my lowest points in my life while I was with my daughter on a mission trip to The Dominican Republic. It was during that trip that God revealed to me the true meaning of grace, but before that moment, I experienced what it felt like to have others carry my burden and help me endure.

One evening, before God spoke to me on my inflated blow up mattress, we were gathered in the courtyard of the home where we were staying. Each night, we'd gather to worship and share about our experiences that day. I honestly didn't feel like worshiping or sharing. I just sat in the back away from the group. It was an awkward experience. I was the Pastor and the one everyone looks to for leadership and encouragement. I had none to give. As the group sang and shared, I sunk my head into my folded arms on the picnic table and began to cry. My soul was dry and empty. I wanted to just walk away from it all. Then, I felt a hand on my shoulder and heard a friend start to pray for me. Then another hand and another voice joined in. Before long, I was surrounded by a group of caring friends who were carrying my burden and lifting me up in prayer. It was beautiful and it was humbling. My pride and my fear of being vulnerable came crashing down as the body of Christ loved on me. It was the next day that God spoke to me on that mattress. I have no doubt it was the prayers of my caring community that gave me the endurance to push deeper and experience God's loving affirmation. Caring communities help you endure when you are ready to give up.

Caring communities also give encouragement. I love the word *encouragement*. Right in the middle of the word is the word "courage." The encouragement that helps us move forward is the kind that gives you the courage to do difficult things. We all need people in our lives that believe in us and breathe courage into us. It's through encouraging words that caring communities restore us when we've failed.

In the middle of writing this section, I received a phone call from a friend inviting me to lunch. Over lunch, my friend shared with me that his wife had just told him she wants a divorce. He's hurting. He's broken. He feels like a loser but he had enough wisdom to reach out to me and invite me to help carry his burden. Over lunch, he shared that earlier that morning, he made a list of people who gave him life and who were encouragers in his life. He said more than ever, he needed those type of people in his life. As we sat and talked, I helped carry his burden by giving counsel and breathing courage into him. He teared up several times when he shared his pain, and each time, I'd breathe into him words of encouragement.

We all need people who breathe courage into us and help us carry our burden. If you are isolating yourself, you are on a long road to recovery. The best indicator of how well someone recovers from a failure is social interaction.

Here's what you can do to allow others to help carry your burden. First, make a list of the people who give you life. Who are the people that breathe courage and hope into you? Write them down. If you can't think of anyone, then you might need some new friends.

One of the best places to start to find encouraging friends is in a church. However, if you just attend a worship service, you'll not make any close friends. Move beyond just attending a church and actually pursue people in smaller groups where you get to know people and you can share your burden. Churches are full of broken people just like you. If you find a church where people aren't honest about their failures, then move on. Find a church where people understand there's only one perfect person and His name is Jesus. Find a place of grace. Press into people and you'll start to heal.

After you have written a list of friends that give your life, then ask for help. Open up about your failure and invite them to pour into you. People want to help. People want to help carry burdens if they can.

Third, let people help you. You can't carry your burdens alone. You were meant to be in community. If people offer to help, let them. If people offer you hope, believe them. If people give you courage, accept it. Healing is a community project. It's time to start healing with others.

QUESTIONS

1. Why is it hard for you to be open with others about your failures?

2. What good could come from connecting to a caring community who will help you bounce back from your failure?

3. Where could you look or who could you ask to find information about a community who could help you walk through what you are going through?

CONCLUSION

So, maybe you feel like the middle school kid who has been punched in the gut. You are hunched over, crying and hating life. Your failure has knocked the breath right out of you and you are wondering if you can move on.

You need to know you aren't finished. We all fail. Yes, every one of us. However, you don't have to let your failures define your future. You can choose the path of Peter or the path of Judas—death or life! You can let God use your failure to remove the rocks in your character and develop you into the man or woman He wants you to be, or you have another choice. You can choose to be finished. The good news is, your failure does not equal finished.

You have a vital part in your future. You can believe the lies and the false labels about who you are or you can believe the truth about who God says you are. You can choose to turn around, change the beliefs and behavior that led to your failure. You can connect to a caring community and find healing. God still has a plan and a purpose for your life. Let Him redeem you, reshape you and refine you for His purpose. Thank God your failure does not equal finished!

I encourage you to not stay down. Get up! Keep moving. God's not finished with you. You still have a future and a purpose. My prayer for you is that you'll allow God's grace to work in your life and let Him give you a renewed love for Him and your life. Use your pain to help others and please share what you've learned through your failure with others.

The purpose of this book is to help people find hope, peace and purpose after they've failed. If this book has helped you, please share it with others. If you feel led, lead a group study through this book and help others find freedom too.

Thank you for investing your time and your resources in this book. This book and you have been prayed for more times than you can imagine. I will continue to pray for you as you allow this book to transform your life.

APPENDIX A:

WHO I AM IN CHRIST

The following is a list of scriptures that describe your true identity as a follower of Jesus. It is not a complete list of all the Bible says about you, but it is a great list to help you change the way you see yourself. Take the time to read through the list and meditate on what each verse says about your true identity. You can use the list as a tool to help you renew your mind by selecting a verse per day or a verse per week to memorize. Use the "I am" statements to declare your true identity. Say them out loud and write them down. As you think about the verse, ask God to help you see yourself as He sees you and to expose any lies you've believed about your identity.

I am a new creation.
Therefore, if anyone is in Christ, he is a new creation. The old has passed away; behold, the new has come. 2 Corinthians 5:17 ESV

I am born again.
Since you have been born again, not of perishable seed but of imperishable, through the living and abiding word of God; 1 Peter 1:23 ESV

I am royalty.

But you are a chosen race, a royal priesthood, a holy nation, a people for his own possession, that you may proclaim the excellencies of him who called you out of darkness into his marvelous light. **1 Peter 2:9** *ESV*

I am uniquely created by God.

For we are his workmanship, created in Christ Jesus for good works, which God prepared beforehand, that we should walk in them. Ephesians 2:10 ESV

I am no longer condemned.

There is therefore now no condemnation for those who are in Christ Jesus. Romans 8:1 ESV

I am a child of God.

But to all who did receive him, who believed in his name, he gave the right to become children of God, John 1:12 ESV

I am righteous.

For our sake he made him to be sin who knew no sin, so that in him we might become the righteousness of God. 2 Corinthians 5:21 ESV

I am the temple of the Holy Spirit.

Or do you not know that your body is a temple of the Holy Spirit within you, whom you have from God? You are not your own, 1 Corinthians 6:19 ESV

I am united with Jesus.

I am the vine; you are the branches. Whoever abides in me and I in him, he it is that bears much fruit, for apart from me you can do nothing. John 15:5 ESV

I am able to take control of my thoughts.

Do not be conformed to this world, but be transformed by the renewal of your mind, that by testing you may discern what is the will of God, what is good and acceptable and perfect. Romans 12:2 ESV

I am not bound by fear.

For God gave us a spirit not of fear but of power and love and self-control. 2 Timothy 1:7 ESV

I am God's friend.

No longer do I call you servants, for the servant does not know what his master is doing; but I have called you friends, for all that I have heard from my Father I have made known to you. John 15:15 ESV

I am a part of God's body.

Now you are the body of Christ and individually members of it. 1 Corinthians 12:27 ESV

I am a citizen of heaven.

But our citizenship is in heaven, and from it we await a Savior, the Lord Jesus Christ, Philippians 3:20 ESV

I am at peace with God.

Therefore, since we have been justified by faith, we have peace with God through our Lord Jesus Christ. Romans 5:1 ESV

I am a part of God's divine nature.

By which he has granted to us his precious and very great promises, so that through them you may become partakers of the divine nature, having escaped from the corruption that is in the world because of sinful desire. 2 Peter 1:4 ESV

I am a child of light.

For you are all children of light, children of the day. We are not of the night or of the darkness. 1 Thessalonians 5:5 ESV

I am bought with a price.

For you were bought with a price. So glorify God in your body. 1 Corinthians 6:20 ESV

I am fearfully and wonderfully made.

I praise you, for I am fearfully and wonderfully made. Wonderful are your works; my soul knows it very well. Psalm 139:14 ESV

I am saved by faith and not by my own good works.

For by grace you have been saved through faith. And this is not your own doing; it is the gift of God, not a result of works, so that no one may boast. Ephesians 2:8-9 ESV

I am crucified with Christ.

I have been crucified with Christ. It is no longer I who live, but Christ who lives in me. And the life I now live in the flesh I live by faith in the Son of God, who loved me and gave himself for me. Galatians 2:20 ESV

I am an ambassador for Christ.

Therefore, we are ambassadors for Christ, God making his appeal through us. We implore you on behalf of Christ, be reconciled to God. 2 Corinthians 5:20 ESV

I am seated with Jesus in heaven.

And raised us up with him and seated us with him in the heavenly places in Christ Jesus, Ephesians 2:6 ESV

I am chosen by God.

You did not choose me, but I chose you and appointed you that you should go and bear fruit and that your fruit should abide, so that whatever you ask the Father in my name, he may give it to you. John 15:16 ESV

I am able to do all things through Christ.

I can do all things through him who strengthens me. Philippians 4:13 ESV

I am a work of God.

And I am sure of this, that he who began a good work in you will bring it to completion at the day of Jesus Christ. Philippians 1:6 ESV

I am set free from sin.

And, having been set free from sin, have become slaves of righteousness. Romans 6:18 ESV

I am empowered by the Holy Spirit.

But you will receive power when the Holy Spirit has come upon you, and you will be my witnesses in Jerusalem and in all Judea and Samaria, and to the end of the earth." Acts 1:8 ESV

I am the light of the world.

"You are the light of the world. A city set on a hill cannot be hidden. Matthew 5:14 ESV

I am the aroma of Christ.

For we are the aroma of Christ to God among those who are being saved and among those who are perishing, 2 Corinthians 2:15 ESV

I am able to approach God with confidence.

Let us then with confidence draw near to the throne of grace, that we may receive mercy and find grace to help in time of need. Hebrews 4:16 ESV

I am adopted by God.

He predestined us for adoption as sons through Jesus Christ, according to the purpose of his will, I am free from the power of darkness. Ephesians 1:5 ESV

I am set free from darkness.

He has delivered us from the domain of darkness and transferred us to the kingdom of his beloved Son, Colossians 1:13 ESV

I am redeemed and forgiven.

In him we have redemption through his blood, the forgiveness of our trespasses, according to the riches of his grace, which he lavished upon us, in all wisdom and insight. Ephesians 1:7-8 ESV

I am sealed by God.

And who has also put his seal on us and given us his Spirit in our hearts as a guarantee. 2 Corinthians 1:22 ESV

I am God's fellow worker.

For we are God's fellow workers. You are God's field, God's building. 1 Corinthians 3:9 ESV

I am favored by God.

For I know the plans I have for you, declares the LORD, plans for welfare and not for evil, to give you a future and a hope. Jeremiah 29:11 ESV

I am saved.

Because, if you confess with your mouth that Jesus is Lord and believe in your heart that God raised him from the dead, you will be saved. Romans 10:9 ESV

I am dead to my old self.

For you have died, and your life is hidden with Christ in God. Colossians 3:3 ESV

I am set aside for God.

And he died for all, that those who live might no longer live for themselves but for him who for their sake died and was raised. 2 Corinthians 5:15 ESV

I am confident God is working all things for my good.

And we know that for those who love God all things work together for good, for those who are called according to his purpose. Romans 8:28 ESV

I am deeply loved by God.

But God shows his love for us in that while we were still sinners, Christ died for us. Romans 5:8 ESV

I am holy and blameless.

He has now reconciled in his body of flesh by his death, in order to present you holy and blameless and above reproach before him, Colossians 1:22 ESV

I am anointed by God.

And it is God who establishes us with you in Christ, and has anointed us, 2 Corinthians 1:21 ESV

ABOUT THE AUTHOR

Randall Popham is the Lead Pastor of Lanier Hills Church in Gainesville, GA and has served in church ministry since 1995. Randall is a graduate of North Greenville University in Greenville, SC and Southern Seminary in Louisville, KY. Randall has been married to his high school sweetheart, Dana, since 1994. They have four children. Randall is also an accomplished artist with pieces of art in several collections.

You can find Randall and Dana Popham online on most Social Media. Randall's email is randall.popham@gmail.com

NOTES

WELCOME TO THE CLUB

1 "Quote by J.M. Barrie: "We are all failures- at least the best of us are."." n.d. https://www.goodreads.com/quotes/288278-we-are-all-failures--at-least-the-best-of-us.

FAILURE IS UNIVERSAL

1 "Romans 3:10 NIV - As It is Written: "There is No One." Bible Gateway. Accessed July 18, 2017. https://www.biblegateway.com/passage/?search=Romans+3%3A10&version=NIV.

WHAT IS FAILURE

1 "Define Failure Search." Google. Accessed July 18, 2017. https://www.google.com/search?q=define+failure&spell=1&sa=X&ved=0ahUKEwjix-zm_pPVAhUM7yYKHSYbCtMQvwUIJSgA&biw=1256&bih=699.

2 "Romans 3:10 NIV - As It is Written: "There is No One." Bible Gateway. Accessed July 18, 2017. https://www.biblegateway.com/passage/?search=Romans+3%3A10&version=NIV.

YOUR BROKEN HEART

1 Winch Ph.D., Guy (2013-07-25). Emotional First Aid: Healing Rejection, Guilt, Failure, and Other Everyday Hurts (p. 173). Penguin Group US. Kindle Edition.

2 "Proverbs 4:23 NIV - Above All Else, Guard Your Heart, for." Bible Gateway. Accessed July 19, 2017. https://www.biblegateway.com/passage/?search=Proverbs+4%3A23&version=NIV.

3 "Psalms 34:18 NIV - The LORD is Close to the Brokenhearted." Bible Gateway. Accessed July 19, 2017. https://www.biblegateway.com/passage/?search=Psalms+34%3A18&version=NIV

4 "The Difference Between Average People and Achieving People is Their Perception of and Response to Failure. - John C. Maxwell." BrainyQuote. Accessed July 19, 2017. https://www.brainyquote.com/quotes/quotes/j/johncmaxw600862.html.

GETTING BACK UP

1 "Proverbs 24:16 NLT - The Godly May Trip Seven Times, but." Bible Gateway. Accessed July 19, 2017. https://www.biblegateway.com/passage/?search=Proverbs+24%3A16&version=NLT.

FAILURE'S DECEPTION

1 "Failure." Ziglar Inc. Accessed July 19, 2017. https://www.ziglar.com/quotes/failure-is-a-detour-not-a-dead-end-street/.

HURT EGO. VULNERABLE MIND

1 "Lamentations 3:22-23 ESV - The Steadfast Love of the LORD Never." Bible Gateway. Accessed July 19, 2017. https://www.biblegateway.com/passage/?search=Lamentations+3%3A22-23&version=ESV.

AGREEING WITH THE ENEMY

1 "Ephesians 6:12 NIV - For Our Struggle is Not Against Flesh." Bible Gateway. Accessed July 19, 2017. https://www.biblegateway.com/passage/?search=Ephesians+6%3A12&version=NIV.

2 "John 10:10 NIV - The Thief Comes Only to Steal and Kill." Bible Gateway. Accessed July 19, 2017. https://www.biblegateway.com/passage/?search=John+10%3A10&version=NIV.

3 "John 8:44 NIV - You Belong to Your Father, the Devil,." Bible Gateway. Accessed July 19, 2017. https://www.biblegateway.com/passage/?search=John+8%3A44&version=NIV.

4 "1 Peter 5:8 NIV - Be Alert and of Sober Mind. Your Enemy." Bible Gateway. Accessed July 19, 2017. https://www.biblegateway.com/passage/?search=1+Peter+5%3A8&version=NIV.

IF YOU THINK YOU'RE FINISHED

1 Winch, Guy. "The Essential Guide for Recovering From Failure." Psychology Today. Accessed July 19, 2017. https://www.psychologytoday.com/blog/the-squeaky-wheel/201307/the-essential-guide-recovering-failure.

2 "Philippians 3:12-14 TLB - I Don't Mean to Say I Am Perfect. I." Bible Gateway. Accessed July 19, 2017. https://www.biblegateway.com/passage/?search=Phili ppians+3%3A12-14&version=TLB.

GOD'S VIEW OF FAILURE

1 "Romans 8:28 NIV - And We Know That in All Things God." Bible Gateway. Accessed July 19, 2017. https://www.biblegateway.com/passage/?search=Rom ans+8%3A28&version=NIV.

2 "Isaiah 55:8,9 NIV - "For My Thoughts Are Not Your." Bible Gateway. Accessed July 19, 2017. https://www.biblegateway.com/passage/?search=Isaia h+55%3A8%2C9&version=NIV.

THE GOD OF FAILURES

1 Hyles, Jack. "Quote by Jack Hyles: "Failing is Not a Disgrace Unless You Make It Th..."." Goodreads. Accessed August 25, 2017. https://www.goodreads.com/quotes/316118-failing-is-not-a-disgrace-unless-you-make-it-the.

TWO FAILURES. TWO DIFFERENT OUTCOMES

1 "Matt 26:33 NIV - Peter Replied, "Even if All Fall Away." Bible Gateway. Accessed August 25, 2017. https://www.biblegateway.com/passage/?search=Matt +26%3A33&version=NIV.

2 "Matt 27:3 NIV - When Judas, Who Had Betrayed Him, Saw." Bible Gateway. Accessed August 25, 2017. https://www.biblegateway.com/passage/?search=matt +27%3A3&version=NIV.

JESUS LOVES FAILURES

1 "Matthew 23:27-28 NIV - "Woe to You, Teachers of the
Law and." Bible Gateway. Accessed August 25, 2017.
https://www.biblegateway.com/passage/?search=Matt
hew+23%3A27-28&version=NIV.

2 "Romans 5:8 NIV - But God Demonstrates His Own Love
for." Bible Gateway. Accessed August 25, 2017.
https://www.biblegateway.com/passage/?search=Rom
ans+5%3A8&version=NIV.

3 "2 Cor 5:21 NIV - God Made Him Who Had No Sin to Be
Sin." Bible Gateway. Accessed August 25, 2017.
https://www.biblegateway.com/passage/?search=2+C
or+5%3A21&version=NIV.

4 "John 1:12 NIV - Yet to All Who Did Receive Him, to."
Bible Gateway. Accessed August 25, 2017.
https://www.biblegateway.com/passage/?search=John
+1%3A12&version=NIV.

GOOD FROM BAD

1 "Assorted Authors About Blessings : We Failed, but in the
Good Providence." Global Christian Quotes. Accessed
August 25, 2017.
http://www.globalchristianquotes.com/quote/172/38.

NOTHING LEFT TO TRY

1 Tchivivdjian, Tullian. *Jesus + Nothing = Everything*, 24.
Crossway, 2011. Kindle.

2 "Colossians 1:12 NIV - and Giving Joyful Thanks to the Father,." Bible Gateway. Accessed August 25, 2017. https://www.biblegateway.com/passage/?search=Colossians+1%3A12&version=NIV.

GETTING WHAT YOU DON'T DESERVE

1 "Forgive | Definition of Forgive by Merriam-Webster." Dictionary by Merriam-Webster: America's Most-trusted Online Dictionary. Accessed August 25, 2017. https://www.merriam-webster.com/dictionary/forgive.

2 "Quote by Dietrich Bonhoeffer: "Costly Grace is the Gospel Which Must Be Sought...."." Goodreads. Accessed August 25, 2017. https://www.goodreads.com/quotes/300616-costly-grace-is-the-gospel-which-must-be-sought-again.

THE DARKROOM

1 "2 Corinthians 4:17 NIV - For Our Light and Momentary Troubles." Bible Gateway. Accessed August 25, 2017. https://www.biblegateway.com/passage/?search=2+Corinthians+4%3A17&version=NIV.

2 "Prosperity Theology - Wikipedia." Wikipedia, the Free Encyclopedia. Accessed August 25, 2017. https://en.wikipedia.org/wiki/Prosperity_theology.

3 Duguid, Barbara. *Extravagant Grace: God's Glory Displayed in Our Weakness*, 149-150. P&R Publishing, 2013. Kindle Edition.

THE POTTER'S WHEEL

1 "Reclaim | Define Reclaim at Dictionary.com."
Dictionary.com. Accessed August 25, 2017.
http://www.dictionary.com/browse/reclaim.

BOUNCE BACK

1 "How High You Bounce." Ziglar Inc. Accessed
August 25, 2017. https://www.ziglar.com/quotes/its-
not-how-far-you-fall/.

EXPECT THE BEST

1 Big Daddy Weave. "Redeemed." CD. Word Music LLC,
Weave Country. 2011.

2 "Hebrews 11:1 NIV - Faith in Action - Now Faith is." Bible
Gateway. Accessed September 1, 2017.
https://www.biblegateway.com/passage/?search=Heb
rews+11%3A1&version=NIV.

3 "Define Optimism Search." Google. Accessed
September 1, 2017.
https://www.google.com/search?q=define+optimism&
oq=define+optimism&aqs=chrome..69i57j0l5.11983j0j4&s
ourceid=chrome&ie=UTF-8.

SELF-COMPASSION

1 Germer, Christopher. "To Recover from Failure, Try Some
Self-Compassion." Harvard Business Review. Accessed
September 1, 2017. https://hbr.org/2017/01/to-recover-
from-failure-try-some-self-compassion.

2 Neff, Kristin. *Self-Compassion: The Proven Power of Being
Kind to Yourself.* NY, NY: William Morrow, 2015.

3 "Mark 12:31 NIV - The Second is This: 'Love Your." Bible Gateway. Accessed September 1, 2017. https://www.biblegateway.com/passage/?search=Mark+12%3A31&version=NIV.

4 "Hebrews 10:12 NIV - But when This Priest Had Offered for." Bible Gateway. Accessed September 1, 2017. https://www.biblegateway.com/passage/?search=Hebrews+10%3A12&version=NIV.

5 "Hebrews 10:14 NIV - For by One Sacrifice He Has Made." Bible Gateway. Accessed September 1, 2017. https://www.biblegateway.com/passage/?search=Hebrews+10%3A14.

6 "Proverbs 12:18 NIV - The Words of the Reckless Pierce Like." Bible Gateway. Accessed September 1, 2017. https://www.biblegateway.com/passage/?search=Proverbs+12%3A18.

REVIVER

1 "Revive Definition Search." Google. Accessed September 1, 2017. https://www.google.com/search?q=revive+definition&oq=revive+d&aqs=chrome.1.69i57j0l2j69i60j0l2.3371j0j4&sourceid=chrome&ie=UTF-8).

2 "Isaiah 57:15 NIV - For This is What the High and Exalted." Bible Gateway. Accessed September 1, 2017. https://www.biblegateway.com/passage/?search=Isaiah+57%3A15&version=NIV.

3 "Luke 15:20 NIV - So He Got Up and Went to His Father." Bible Gateway. Accessed September 1, 2017. https://www.biblegateway.com/passage/?search=Luke+15%3A20&version=NIV.

4 "Luke 15:21 NIV - "The Son Said to Him, 'Father, I." Bible Gateway. Accessed September 1, 2017. https://www.biblegateway.com/passage/?search=Luke+15%3A21&version=NIV.

5 "Repent | Definition of Repent by Merriam-Webster." Dictionary by Merriam-Webster: America's Most-trusted Online Dictionary. Accessed September 1, 2017. https://www.merriam-webster.com/dictionary/repent.

6 "Luke 15:22-24 NIV - "But the Father Said to His Servants," Bible Gateway. Accessed September 1, 2017. https://www.biblegateway.com/passage/?search=Luke+15%3A22-24&version=NIV.

7 "Romans 8:35-39 NIV - Who Shall Separate Us from the Love of." Bible Gateway. Accessed September 1, 2017. https://www.biblegateway.com/passage/?search=Romans+8%3A35-39&version=NIV.

8 "Acts 3:19 NIV - Repent, Then, and Turn to God, So That." Bible Gateway. Accessed September 1, 2017. https://www.biblegateway.com/passage/?search=Acts+3%3A19&version=NIV.

LABELS

1 "Proverbs 4:23 NIV - Above All Else, Guard Your Heart, for." Bible Gateway. Accessed September 1, 2017. https://www.biblegateway.com/passage/?search=Proverbs+4%3A23&version=NIV.

2 "Ephesians 1:16-19 NIV - I Have Not Stopped Giving Thanks for." Bible Gateway. Accessed September 1, 2017. https://www.biblegateway.com/passage/?search=Ephesians+1%3A16-19&version=NIV.

3 "James 1:5 NIV - If Any of You Lacks Wisdom, You Should." Bible Gateway. Accessed September 1, 2017.

https://www.biblegateway.com/passage/?search=Jame
s+1%3A5&version=NIV

YOUR PURPOSE

1 "2 Corinthians 12:9 NIV - But He Said to Me, "My Grace
   is." Bible Gateway. Accessed September 1, 2017.
   https://www.biblegateway.com/passage/?search=2+C
   orinthians+12%3A9&version=NIV.

A HEALING COMMUNITY

1 "Galatians 6:2 NIV - Carry Each Other's Burdens, and in."
   Bible Gateway. Accessed September 1, 2017.
   https://www.biblegateway.com/passage/?search=Gala
   tians+6%3A2&version=NIV.

2 "G941 - Bastaz_ - Strong's Greek Lexicon (KJV)." Blue
   Letter Bible. Accessed September 1, 2017.
   https://www.blueletterbible.org/lang/lexicon/lexicon.
   cfm?Strongs=G941&t=KJV.

3 "Romans 15:5 NIV - May the God Who Gives Endurance
   and." Bible Gateway. Accessed September 1, 2017.
   https://www.biblegateway.com/passage/?search=Rom
   ans+15%3A5&version=NIV.

Made in the USA
Columbia, SC
02 February 2018